Now that I Come to Die

Now that I Come to Die
Intimate guidance from one of Tibet's greatest masters

Longchenpa

Introduction by Tarthang Tulku

DHARMA PUBLISHING

Tibetan Translation Series

Copyright © 2007 Dharma Publishing
All rights reserved. No part of this book,
either text or art, may be reproduced or stored digitally
or in any other format without written permission.
For information, contact
2425 Hillside Ave., Berkeley, California, 94704 USA

Edited by the staff of Dharma Publishing
Typeset in Spectrum
Printed and bound in the United States of America
by Dharma Press, California
Design and layout by Kando Dorsey
Library of Congress Control Number 2007922400
ISBN 13: 978-0-89800-393-2

Dharma Publishing is also the publisher of
Longchenpa's *Kindly Bent to Ease Us*, vols 1–3.

9 8 7 6 5 4 3 2 1

All beings are transients, like past and future guests:
The old have gone; the young will also go.
This generation will not even last a hundred years —
Understand this thoroughly straight away.

Contents

Introduction: All Knowledge, All Light   Tarthang Tulku
9

Now that I Come to Die — Longchenpa's Parting Injunctions
41

The Four Immeasurably Great Catalysts of Being
67

Longchenpa's Verses and Commentary on
The Four Immeasurably Great Catalysts of Being
87

Notes
125

Longchenpa Sadhana
129

Bibliography
134

Acknowledgments
139

Index
141

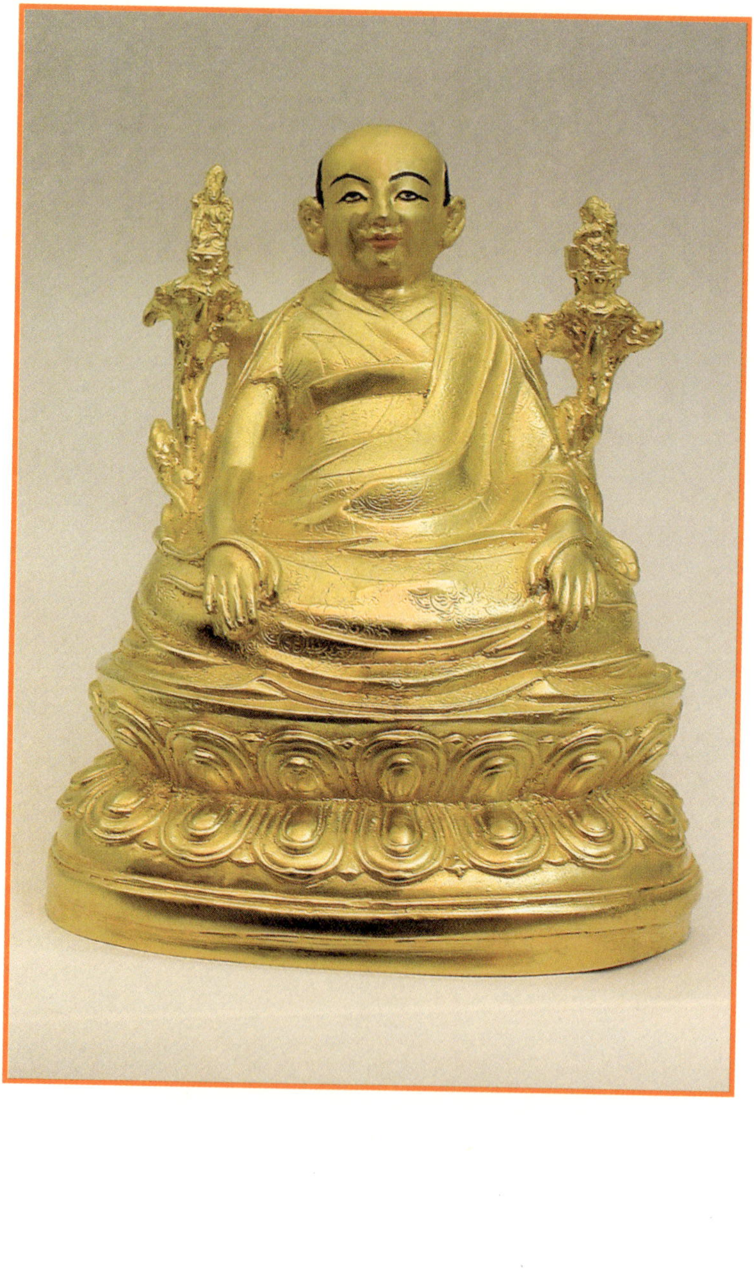

Introduction

All Knowledge, All Light

In the eighth century of the common era, three revered masters fulfilled an ancient vow to bring the Buddha's teachings to the Land of Snow. These great beings are known as the Three Founding Fathers: Guru Padmasambhava from the kingdom of Oddiyana, master of Mantrayana; Abbot Shantarakshita from the great Indian university of Nalanda, master of Sutrayana; and the Tibetan King Trisong Detsun, regarded as an incarnation of the Great Bodhisattva Manjushri, who invited the Dharma into his kingdom and lent it royal support.

Thus the oldest tradition of Tibetan Buddhism, the Nyingma School, was established. It was a most auspicious time, as the Dharma was in full flower in its original homeland of India, and the complete range of teachings could be transmitted in all their depth and vastness. From these early foundations the Nyingma tradition has continued uninterrupted for over twelve centuries. Despite the recent disruption of Tibetan civilization, its lineages survive unbroken even today, both inside and outside Tibet.

Nearly six hundred years after the time of the Founding Fathers, in 1308, at a time when the Nyingma school was thriving and new schools had been founded, the omniscient (Kunkyen) Longchen Rabjam came into the world. This incomparable master, known also as Drime Odzer, or simply as Longchenpa, is widely considered the most important explicator of the Dzogchen teachings of the Nyingma school. His writings and teachings, as well as the example of his life, have had an immense impact on Dharma practitioners for over seven centuries.

The Nyingma tradition, of which Longchenpa is a major exemplar, envisions nine vehicles or Yanas leading to the complete enlightenment of a Buddha. The first three Yanas are the Shravakayana, Pratyekabuddhayana, and Bodhisattvayana. The first two focus on the teachings found in the Buddha's First Turning of the Wheel of the Dharma, while the third, the Bodhisattvayana, embraces all three Turnings of the Wheel.

The remaining six Yanas are based on the teachings of the Tantras. The three Outer Tantras are the Kriya, Charya, and Yoga Tantras. Hundreds of works related to these teachings are gathered in the Kanjur and Tanjur (the spoken word of the Buddha and their commentaries), including the Tantras followed by the Sarma or New Schools.

The three Inner Tantras, the Mahayoga, Anuyoga and Atiyoga, are the highest of the nine Yanas. They are preserved and transmitted only within the Nyingma tradition. These teachings are transmitted from the Adibuddha through Vajrasattva and the great Bodhisattvas into the human realm. Handed down in India for centuries under conditions of great secrecy, the Inner Tantras were brought into Tibet in the era of the Three Founding Fathers.

Atiyoga (known also as Mahasandhi, or in Tibetan as Dzogchen) is the ninth Yana, the highest of the three Inner Yoga Tantras. Atiyoga has its own view (tawa), practice (gompa), and action manifestation (shopa). The view is based on enlightenment itself. It is the nature of Dharmakaya as symbolized by the Buddha Samantabhadra (known in inadequate translation as the Primordial Enlightened One). The practice is the enlightened transmission of Dharmakaya from one fully realized master to the next. The action manifestation is teaching in accord with the needs of nine kinds of audience. The Atiyoga teachings are preserved in the collection known as The Hundred Thousand Tantras (Gyud Bum), which encompasses the million topics of all three of the Inner Tantras.

The transmission lineage of the Atiyoga passes from the Dharmakaya to the Sambhogakaya through the Buddha Vajrasattva. It enters the human realm through Garab Dorje (first century CE). His disciple, Manjushrimitra, passed on the teachings to Shri Simha, who in turn bestowed them upon Vimalamitra, Jnanasutra, Guru Padmasambhava and Lochen Vairotsana (who also received visionary teachings directly from Garab Dorje). Together with the master Buddhaguhya, who trained countless disciples in the Mahayoga teachings from his dwelling place on Mount Kailash, these teachers – Padmasambhava, Vimalamitra, and Vairotsana – were instrumental in bringing the Inner Yogas to the Land of Snow.

In the early days of the Dharma in Tibet, the Atiyoga teachings were transmitted in secret, and few people even knew about them. This is because the teachings of the esoteric Inner Tantras proceed from the highest enlightened view of the Dharmakaya, and for those not ready for them, they are easy to misunderstand. Even those well versed in the Dharma may encounter this difficulty. Training in the traditions of the lower Yanas emphasizes certain specific doctrines (for example, the central importance of mind and consciousness, the role of karma and klesha, the workings of cause and effect, and the operation of past, present, and future). Scholars of Madhyamika, Abhidharma, and even Prajnaparamita tend to have commitments of one kind or another to such doctrines, which make it easy for them to misinterpret Atiyoga teachings. Therefore, the Atiyoga teachings were closely guarded during the period when the Dharma was gradually introduced to the Tibetan people.

As part of the comprehensive Dharma transmission to the Land of Snow, three major transmission lineages for the Atiyoga were founded. The first lineage is that of Padmasambhava, who transmitted the teachings to some of his twenty-five chief disciples, such as Gyelmo Yudra Nyingpo, Kawa Peltsek, Chogro Lui Gyeltsen, Nyak Jnanakumara, and Nubchen Sangye Yeshe. The second transmission lineage originates with Vairotsana, who transmitted it to his five most important students: Gyelmo Yudra Nyingpo, Sangton Yeshe Lama, Pangen Sangye Gonpo, Nyak Jnanakumara, and Lady Sherab Dronma of Khotan. Finally Vimalamitra conferred the third transmission lineage of Atiyoga teachings on his five principal disciples: Trisong Detsun, Prince Mune Tsenpo, Nyang Ting nge dzin, Kawa Peltsek, and Chogro Lui Gyeltsen. These three major transmissions all continued intact until the time of Longchenpa.

Two Streams of Transmission

Longchenpa is considered the reincarnation of two individuals from this early period of transmission who each played a key role in the transmission of the Atiyoga teachings: the great sage Vimalamitra, and Princess Pema Sel, the daughter of King Trisong Detsun. As the karmic connections made at this time ripened in his person, Longchenpa was able to unite the Atiyoga lineages passed down through Padmasambhava and through Vimalamitra.

Vimalamitra was born in Kashmir, an emanation of Manjushri. On his many travels he taught at Nalanda and Bodh Gaya, in Bengal, in Kashmir, and in central India. At the time when Trisong Detsun took the throne in Tibet, Vimalamitra was residing in Oddiyana as the head of five hundred Mahapanditas, or great learned masters.

Having previously received Dzogchen teachings from Lochen Vairotsana, King Trisong Detsun sent emissaries to Oddiyana to invite Vimalamitra to Tibet to receive further instruction, for he had been told that this master was holder of countless enlightened lineages of the Mantrayana and Sutrayana. When the Kashmiri master arrived, however, Vairotsana had been exiled to the remote region of Gyelmo Rong, as a result of intrigues by courtiers who had succeeded in convincing the king that his teachings were false. Under these circumstances, Vimalamitra at first chose to keep the Inner Tantras a secret. When he eventually revealed them to the king, Trisong Detsun realized that Vairotsana's teachings were very similar, and he hastily invited Vairotsana to return from exile.

Vimalamitra stayed in Tibet for thirteen years, practicing intensively at the monastery of Samye, in Lhasa, and at other holy places and retreat centers. He transmitted, translated, and concealed for future discovery various texts on the Inner Tantras, including the works known collectively as the Vima Nying-tig. (Although these are esoteric terms with very precise meanings, in general the term 'nying-tig' refers to the heart of the heart, the center of all enlightened knowledge; literally, 'nying' means 'heart' and 'tig' means 'drop.')

From Tibet, Vimalamitra traveled to Mount Wu-t'ai-shan in China, a mountain closely associated with the Mahabodhisattva Manjushri. He chose this sacred location to pass away, manifesting the rainbow body and becoming immortal. Great masters and practitioners in later times reported meeting Vimalamitra in their meditations. In one of these spiritual encounters Vimalamitra promised two of his disciples, Chetsun Senge Wangchuk and Dangma Lhungyi Gyeltsen, that he would return to Tibet in an emanation-body once every century. One such emanation was Longchenpa.

Longchenpa's other incarnation lineage traces to Princess Lhachen Pema Sel, the daughter of King Trisong Detsun. At the age of eight, the princess was stung by a bee and died as the result of an allergic reaction. Desolate with grief, the king took his daughter's body to Samye Chimpu, where

Guru Padmasambhava was in residence, and begged for his help. Assisted by his consort Yeshe Tsogyal, the great Guru performed a special ceremony and brought the girl back to life: today a square rock in a cave at Chimpu still commemorates the site of this miracle. Guru Padmasambhava then bestowed on the princess the Atiyoga teachings known as the Khandro Nying-tig, empowering her to reveal these teachings in a future rebirth. Concealed for later discovery, they were found in the thirteenth or fourteenth century by Pema Leytrel tsel, the incarnation of Princess Pema Sel immediately prior to Longchenpa.

Field of Vast Knowledge

Longchenpa was born on March 1, 1308, in the village of Todrung in the Dra Valley, located in the Yoru region of central Tibet. His father, Lopon Tensrung, was the son of a great master and renowned healer named Lhasrung, a descendant of a nephew of one of Padmasambhava's twenty-five chief disciples who lived to be 105 years old. Longchenpa's mother, Sonam Gyen, belonged to the lineage of the sister of Dromtonpa, a disciple of Atisha and a revered figure in the history of the Kadampa School.

Longchenpa's birth was marked by auspicious signs, and Dharmapalas (protectors of the Dharma) appeared to protect and serve him. The young child displayed the character of a noble being and mastered Dharma studies with remarkable ease. By the age of five he had learned to read and write and began his studies, receiving initiations from his father. At the age of nine, he memorized the Prajnaparamita in 25,000 and 8,000 lines, and at the age of twelve he was ordained as a novice. Soon his fame as a scholar-practitioner began to spread, and within a few years he was acknowledged as a master by all Buddhist schools in Tibet. No one could match him in debate, no matter what the subject, for he completely commanded the Sutras and Tantras. In time he became known as Kunkyen Longchenpa, the All-Knowing Vastness Field of Knowledge.

As a practitioner, Longchenpa had countless visions of Buddhas, Bodhisattvas, deities, Dharmapalas, and dakinis. It is said that when he beheld Saraswati, the goddess of learning, she revealed to him in the palm of her hand a vision of all the universes, a vision that Longchenpa contemplated without interruption for seven full days. He had hundreds of students, and he often gave initiations to thousands of practitioners at one time. Great scholars of both the Nyingma and Sarma schools regularly sought his guidance on points of doctrine and practice.

As an author, Longchenpa became renowned for the beauty of his poetry and prose as well as for the clarity of his style. He is credited with more than two hundred works, both as an author and compiler, many of which, including a number of Sutra commentaries, have been lost. The works that survive are counted among the masterpieces of Tibetan literature. Most famous are the sNying-thig Ya-bzhi teachings that bring together the transmission of Vimalamitra and Padmasambhava; the works known as the *Seven Treasures* (mDzod-bdun), *The Trilogy of Natural Freedom* (Rang-grol-skor-gsum), *The Trilogy of Dispelling the Darkness* (Mun-sel-skor-gsum), and *The Trilogy of Finding Comfort and Ease* (Ngal-gso-skor-gsum; published by Dharma Publishing in three volumes as *Kindly Bent to Ease Us*). Each of the three trilogies was provided with commentary by Longchenpa himself. Other texts that have survived the centuries include an extensive Dharma history, a work on logic, and commentaries on the Uttaratantra of Maitreya and the Kunjed Gyalpo Tantra.

Longchenpa spent much of his life in Central Tibet, the region where he was born. In fact he spent so much time at Samye and its retreat center, Samye Chimpu, that he is sometimes known as Samye-pa. He helped rebuild many of the temples at Samye and the retreat centers at Chimpu, and later in his life established and repaired many temples in the land of Bhutan as well. For the most part, however, Longchenpa preferred to live on retreat in remote places, and he became known as an example of a perfect Atiyoga practitioner: the embodiment of Dharmakaya.

Longchenpa's lineage continued through his disciples, including those known as the three accomplished ones, the five spiritual sons, the four spiritual benefactors, and the four accomplished yogins. Not all the Mahayoga and Anuyoga lineages he transmitted remain intact, but his Atiyoga teachings have had a powerful and enduring impact up until today. In later centuries, famous masters became his direct disciples by encountering him in visionary experiences after praying for his blessings. These include Lhatsun Namka Jigme (1597-1650), considered an incarnation of both Vimalamitra and Longchenpa; Kunkyen Terdag Lingpa (1646-1714), an incarnation of Vairotsana; and Kunkyen Jigme Lingpa (1730-1798) also an incarnation of Vimalamitra and Longchenpa. Each of these supremely accomplished masters received Atiyoga teachings from the great master directly in mind to mind transmission. The transmission received by Jigme Lingpa in a series of visions at Chimpu was especially important, for through this transmission Jigme Lingpa thoroughly understood the great ocean of teachings and was able to transmit the cycle of Dzogchen teachings known today as the Longchen Nying-tig.

In later times, countless accomplished masters attained inner realization of the profound Dzogchen teachings through practicing the Nying-tig lineages that Longchenpa united in his being. They included Jamyang Khyentse Wangpo, Patrul Rinpoche, Do Khyentse Yeshe Dorje, Adzom Drugpa, and Jamyang Khyentse Chokyi Lodro.

In the Presence of Kuntuzangpo

However deeply his accomplishments, realizations, and legacy are revered, there is still more to comprehend about why Kunkyen Longchenpa holds such a central place within the Nyingma School. It may be best to say simply that Longchenpa united and perfected in himself all aspects of the enlightened lineages. In mastery of the Sutrayana, he was the equal of Nagarjuna; in mastery of the shastra tradition he was like the six great masters of India; in mastery of the Mantrayana, he was the equal of all the Vidyadharas of the Vajrayana; and in mastery of meditation he was the equal of the great sage Milarepa. He was an honored scholar but also a great siddha, who preferred to dwell in sacred places and mountain caves and celebrated in his writings the beauty of untamed nature. He maintained the perfect discipline of the Great Arhats, and in his actions he so fully exemplified the practice of the Bodhisattvas that he might be regarded as the equal of Avalokiteshvara himself. Terton (treasure finder), pandita, visionary practitioner — Longchenpa is the greatest example of the accomplishments that the Atiyoga lineage offers. His life story offers profound inspiration to all who reflect on it, for it reveals what it is like to live as a perfect master of the teachings.

At the age of fifty-six, having mastered the Dharma realms in the same way a chakravartin king becomes sovereign of the entire world, Longchenpa announced that he had achieved what he had set out to do in this life. Before entering parinirvana, he urged his students to prepare themselves well, taking full advantage of the opportunities that life offers for escaping the bonds of samsara. His teachings on this occasion are the source of the text published here as "Now that I Come to Die."

On January 24, 1364 the master passed into parinirvana. The earth shook several times, and although it was mid-winter, flowers spontaneously erupted and blossomed.

> *Now that the connection with this life has lost its karmic power,*
> *Do not lament about this beggar*
> *Who died happily and unattached,*
> *But constantly pray that he be with you in spirit.*
> — Now that I Come to Die

In his teachings Longchenpa placed a special emphasis on impermanence. With a few well chosen words and the example of his own life, Longchenpa shows how things arise and pass away, revealing that the truth of enlightenment is always at hand. He reminds us that being aware of constant change and the shortness of life is a complete teaching in itself, encouraging us to maximize our time and energy while we still can. Furthermore he constantly advised his students that birth as a human being is rare and precious. Human beings are in fortunate circumstances, for they can practice with all their energy and all their hearts, studying in depth the nature of human awareness. Always reminding his students that intellectual and conceptual knowledge cannot penetrate to the level of enlightenment, Longchenpa teaches that we can see this for ourselves only after understanding how the mind works. On the basis of this understanding, we can embody the Dharmakaya. Having discovered that nirvana is not some distant realm, separate from ordinary experience, we can manifest enlightenment within our own life.

The major traditions of Tibetan Buddhism all have their great exemplars. For example, the Sakyapa honor Sakya Pandita, master of all the scriptures and all knowledge, while the Gelugpa revere Tsongkhapa, master of all the Sutras and Tantras. To the Nyingmapa, Longchenpa's attainments transcend all other attributes. Nothing in this universe is more precious than the teachings he left us, for those who study them perfectly gain direct access to the enlightened realm. His style of writing is profound and striking and his insights in the realm of philosophy, psychology, and practice go beyond those of all others. In his own life and actions he set in motion a dynamic that can penetrate the rigid patterns of our mind, helping us transcend our limitations. The beauty of his teachings and the qualities through which he evokes understanding bring us directly into the presence of the Adibuddha.

The Highest Realization

The highest realization a master in the Dzogchen tradition can achieve is the rainbow body, in which the practitioner attains immortality and leaves no body behind. In early times, Vimalamitra attained the rainbow body, as did several of his direct disciples, though he is also said still to dwell at Mount Wu T'ai Shan. The great Kadampa Deshek (1122-1192), founder of Katok Monastery, established a lineage in which practitioners focused on a more frequently attained goal, in which at the time of passing away the body simply vanishes, leaving behind only hair and nails. According to the meticulous records kept at the monastery close to a hundred thousand practitioners achieved this level of realization over the course of three centuries.

In more recent times, great masters such as Adzom Drukpa (1842-1924), as well as his teacher Jamyang Kyentse'i Wangpo (1820-1892) have attained the rainbow body. When the great

Nyak-la Padma Dudul (1816-1872) felt his life coming to an end, he gathered his disciples around him at a cave at the top of a mountain and entered a small tent to meditate. After seven days of intense practice in which his disciples participated, he vanished. All that remained on the ground where he was sitting were little heaps of his hair and nails. Numerous written accounts of similar accomplishments by other masters, dating from the nineteenth and twentieth centuries, were preserved in eastern Tibet.

Such attainments demonstrate that through practicing Atiyoga, highly advanced practitioners are able to enter the Dharmakaya directly. Having accumulated the necessary karma through meritorious action, their prayers and devotion allow them to communicate directly with the enlightened realm, no longer relying on the human mind. Human beings in turn can communicate with them, from heart to heart, until they learn to see with Dharma eyes. That possibility is what Longchenpa offers us, and that is why these teachings and practices, transmitted by Longchenpa with supreme clarity, have become so well known and highly honored.

ONE WAY TO APPROACH UNDERSTANDING
Rather than seeking explanation for such extraordinary achievements, which the human mind cannot comprehend,

it might be best to pass over such realization in silence. Still, an ordinary, conceptual understanding of these attainments may also be of benefit. Although my views at this level may be mistaken, I offer them here in case others find them helpful.

Suppose that all existence arises 'within' shunyata. If that is so, mind and shunyata are inseparable. To experience this inseparability of mind and shunyata implies union with the dharmadatu, and once there is union with the dharmadhatu, nothing is 'outside'. Everything is included in the enlightened realm: ordinary substance, mind, karma and klesha, cause and effect, and conventional reason. No residues remain; light is everywhere.

Since nothing is outside this realization, the boundaries that appear to separate 'this' from 'that' or 'you' from 'me' no longer have a function. The entire realm of existence is simply appearance, and what appears is inseparable from shunyata. Realization at this level effortlessly transcends relative conceptual existence, giving immediate access to nirvana and enlightenment. In practical terms, this means that realization can be transferred from 'one' consciousness to 'another'.

The great masters of the Dzogchen lineage understand this not only on the theoretical level, but as a living reality. They embody and transmit this reality to others spontaneously. Samsara, karma, and klesha all become part of the enlightened process, a constant transmutation that itself constitutes the path to enlightenment.

At our level of practice and understanding, bridging the gap between samsara and nirvana, between ordinary mind and true realization, seems problematic and difficult. The leap from one realm into the other cannot be understood with the rational mind alone. Yet the difficulty itself arises only within the framework of samsaric logic and thought. From our relative perspective, the operation of karma generates thick clouds that leave us in the dark, unable to perceive reality, see the future, understand the past, or comprehend the nature and dynamic of time. With nothing to go on but ordinary rationality, we rely on relative convictions, which reason, science, and history all confirm.

How does our ordinary mind operate? First we frame a picture of the way we believe things are, and then we live within that frame. Whatever does not fit within the frame is referred to as a mystery: inexplicable, nonsensical, or perhaps supernatural. Concepts such as 'before the beginning', 'after the end', or 'formless form' leave us with no way to respond, speechless and confused.

At the enlightened level, however, the picture frame does not play the same limiting role. Things that scientists and philosophers are unable to explain, the practitioner may discover within practice. For instance, a practitioner may suddenly grasp that form simply 'is' formless: that form and formless are inseparable.

Suppose that mind can exhibit mind to mind, like a story flickering across a television screen. Suppose we had access not only to the story on the screen, but to the technical 'production aspects' that contribute to making the story available. That would bring us closer to the realized perspective. The enlightened ones are perfectly aware that the fiction that unfolds within the frame is unborn and uncreated. In traditional terms, this is called perfect wisdom, Prajnaparamita, or dharmadhatu. If the kaya of dharmadhatu, the body of existence, is pervasive, then whatever arises embodies Dharmakaya. Nothing is left out. There is no inside or outside, no thing and no 'no thing'.

Within our personal picture frame, we continue to make comparisons and distinguish yes from no; we apply our logic of names and labels. But just because it 'makes sense' within the frame does not mean that it is the truth. The ordinary, conventional, samsaric frame of mind has been conditioned to operate in a certain way. Language, thoughts, senses, and the operation of karma and klesha all reflect that design, whose author is human consciousness. Mind designs and frames a picture of a future and a past, and within that frame the truths of human civilization find their place. First there is a point of creation, then a history of mind. Gradually the rhythms of rhythm, the sounds of sound emerge. We develop language, pose questions and discover answers, and experience through the senses. All this presents itself in a way that facilitates agreement, leading to conviction. Reality is established: the domain of relative truth, known in Buddhism as *samvrtti satya*. In dependence on the structures of human consciousness, the three realms – the realm of desire, the realm of form, and the formless realm – come into being.

Even on the conceptual level, we can ask: Why do things work in this way? Why could they not work differently? Could there be a 'higher' realm, a higher truth, one to which we ordinarily have no access with our conceptual mind? Could this be what Western religions refer to when they speak of God, or what Buddhism is pointing toward when it speaks of the enlightened or awakened state, the dharmadhatu, or (at a more philosophical level) of prajna, wisdom, or shunyata? Could such a higher reality be understood as all encompassing, as more comprehensive than the reality framed by human consciousness? In naming such a possibility, do we move closer to that which is not necessarily substance or not-substance, not existence but also not the non-existence of existence? We can acknowledge that such a possibility goes beyond our ability to see or sense it, but that does not mean that it is not there, or that it is not what *is* there.

Acknowledging such possibilities may be helpful, but we are still only speculating. We are still in the realm of language and explanations, concepts and constructs. Even if we glimpse something that seems real, it is at most the tip of the iceberg. It seems we are simply interpreting our own mind, or even the interpretations of our own mind. And when we do that, when we behave like philosophers, we are at best just knocking on the door to other realms, other possibilities. Stuck within the frame, we cannot enter a reality beyond the frame, cannot go deeper into other ways of being or see other dimensions of mind.

That is where the practice of Dzogchen or Atiyoga enters. The Dzogchen way of practice goes beyond mind. It transcends concepts and is not bound by words. As a lineage of realization, it leaves behind ordinary perception. Step by step it lets go of karmic manufacturing and the transmission forward of what is so, of cause leading to effect. It goes beyond all that, goes to a higher level.

But again this is saying too much. 'Higher' and 'lower' make sense only in terms of the relative level of comparisons and constructs. Actually, there is no hierarchy. Once more we see that words are not the right vehicle. We cannot forcefully imagine another way to be, nor can we 'deny' the reality of what we experience. If words were needed, we might speak of 'transcending' or of 'shunyata', but when we do so we are again making use of mind and concepts.

Whenever we perceive, we are the perceiver; whenever we speak, we are the speaker. We are the pursuer and the one who engages the inquiry. The agent of these actions is always the ordinary mind, with its conventional opinions and views, and also with its sense that those opinions and views must be transcended. Even the most sophisticated therapy for samsaric mind remains an interpretation, based on language, concepts, and imagery, on pointing *to* something *from* a particular perspective. That kind of relationship keeps us bound to human patterns and the expression of human consciousness. Whatever its attractions, it is not a great achievement.

The all-knowing Longchenpa, in his life and in his teachings, showed a way out of this trap. He showed how to activate the teachings step by step. He demonstrated that the Sutrayana leads automatically to the Mantrayana and the Tantras, which lead in turn to the essence of the three inner yoga Tantras. He himself is the living embodiment of this realization: Longchenpa, Jnenendra, one with the great enlightened omniscient ones. He is present for us now, his knowledge uniting us with the Dharmakaya.

Those who take a religious view toward life may look for God; those who take a philosophical view may look for truth. Still others may look for love. Whatever they look for — whatever *you* look for — that is Longchenpa. Externally he expresses the blessings of the enlightened lineage. Internally, nothing is left: just the naked, perfect quality of enlightenment.

For all Humanity

How we can love Longchenpa? How can we enter into intimacy with the wisdom and compassion he manifested? His legacy is for all humanity. His whole purpose in appearing in this world is to help beings awaken from samsara, to perfect this universe, to transform and put an end to all misery, suffering, and confusion. Human beings are caught in a nightmare, and Longchenpa is here to rescue them from its grip. The path he teaches can free all beings from hunger and desire, stupidity and confusion, loneliness, hatred, and pain. Seeing through the human condition, we need no longer accept the product of suffering.

Longchenpa invites us to get started on the project of enlightenment. He shows us the steps we need to take to transform our ordinary life into an expression of enlightenment. His teachings illustrate that all elements of conventional experience are building blocks of wisdom: thoughts, concepts, emotions, senses, and feelings. All ordinary things are transcendable and transmutable. There is no need to beat ourselves over the head with our shortcomings or to wallow in guilt. We do not need to claim our identity as the victims of our karma, nor do we need to suffer alone. There is a way out, and that way is perfect enlightenment.

In practicing these teachings we can unite with Longchenpa. The great master invites us home, embodying the best of human potential, accessible to each one of us. By opening our hearts to Longchenpa we receive his blessings, for he embraces us as we are. Longchenpa's love joins with our own. In the exchange we receive his compassion and his awakened energy, loosening the grip of samsara on our minds and hearts.

Reading *Kindly Bent to Ease Us*, the English translation of the Ngal-gso-skor-gsum, offers a small taste of the beauty that Longchenpa makes available. Even though the translation is not completely accurate, the text gives a sense of how Longchenpa encourages the reader to start the journey on the path and of how he sees the nature of samsara. Notice that Longchenpa does not ask us to start by reflecting on the nature of the Buddha's enlightenment. Instead, he asks us to investigate the nature of samsara and of our own confusion. He implores us to do it 'straight away'.

Once we understand something about human nature and the functioning of the mind, we naturally begin to wonder who we really are. How did we come to misunderstand our own being? What is it that we have lost, and how can we return to the wholeness of our being? As these questions become meaningful, we discover that Longchenpa, the 'all-knowing' master, gives us the answers we seek at the level we presently occupy. When we need explanations, he offers them. When we need to satisfy the questions posed by ordinary mind, he offers conventional truths. And when we ask how to wake up, he gives us the necessary practices.

Longchenpa is the master pandita and the peerless psychologist. He knows how to separate mind and wisdom. He stands ready to show us the path that leads to enlightenment and the path that leads to samsara, and how to connect the two. He reveals how to enter the path and engage the teachings, and he explains in detail whatever we need to know as we proceed. He clarifies the nine qualities of mind manifestation, helping us understand others. He unites knowledge, practice, and blessings into a complete teaching and a complete path. Truly he is the incomparable master, the perfect manifestation of the Buddha's sacred realization.

Calling on Longchenpa

Here is a simple practice to connect with the master: Visualize Longchenpa as the Vajra Guru above the crown of your head, either about eighteen inches in height or the size of a human being. Seated on a lotus, he manifests the rainbow body of pure light, both hands resting on his knees. Chant the following mantra (or the Vajra Guru mantra):

Om Ah Hum Vajra Mahaguru Sarvajnana Siddhi Pala Hum

As you chant, regard Longchenpa as a living presence, the omniscient (Sarvajnana) great teacher (Mahaguru). You may wish to reflect that Manjushri is the essence of the knowledge of all the Buddhas, Vimalamitra is the manifestation of Manjushri, and Longchenpa is the incarnation of Vimalamitra.

After chanting for some time, pray silently for union with Longchenpa. Visualize rays of light emanating from his body: white light in the form of the Tibetan letter OM enters the chakra in your forehead; red light in the form of the Tibetan letter AH enters your throat chakra; and blue light in the form of the Tibetan letter HUM enters your heart chakra. As light enters the body, your prayer is granted, and you become inseparable from the mind, teachings, and embodiment of Longchenpa, like water mixing with water.

Repeat this practice two to three times during a single session. Let the enlightened Dharmakaya blessings of Longchenpa become the very essence of your body, mind and spirit. Accept these blessings of joy and love, which are the foundation for miraculous displays (siddhi).

When great masters have practiced in this way with deep devotion, many miracles have happened. If you do the practice with complete confidence, whatever you consider less than perfect will be transformed. Longchenpa's blessings effortlessly overcome the power of the Kaliyuga, transforming your own weaknesses, the obstacles that stand in your way, and the most fearsome and potent displays of the marayas.

—Tarthang Tulku
Odiyan, January 2007

Prayer to Longchenpa

dzamling dzay pay gyen drug chog nyi dang
thuk kyi lung tog nyam pay thug nga wa
nag trod dam par bay pay tul zhug kyi
kor day cho kur dzog pay longchenpa
drimed odzer zhab la sol wa deb

The Six Ornaments and the
Two Most Excellent Ones of the whole world:
The learning and realization of their
enlightened hearts, your heart equals.
Hidden yogi practicing in
sacred forest groves, Longchenpa,
You are the perfect unity of samsara and
nirvana as Dharmakaya:
Drimed Ozer (Immaculate Rays of Light)
at your feet we pray.

Now that I Come to Die

Longchenpa's
parting injunctions

translation, introduction, and annotations by
Herbert V. Guenther

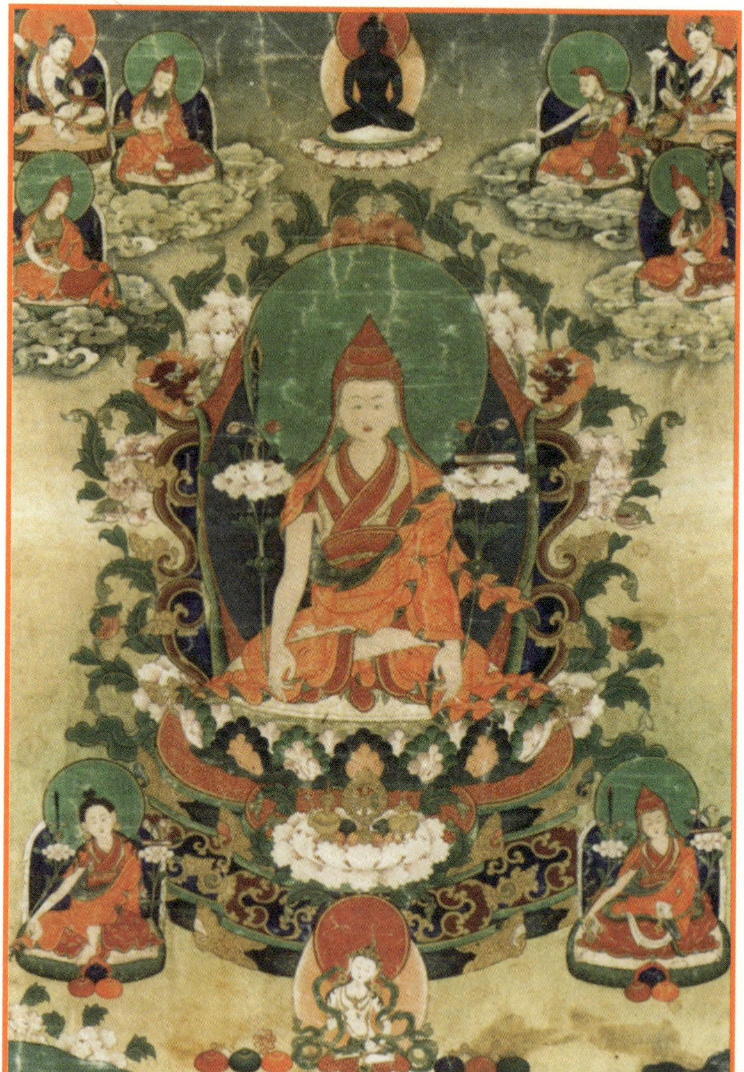

Now that I Come to Die

The year of Klong-chen rab-'byams-pa's (Longchenpa) death is often given as 1363, referring to the beginning of the Tibetan lunar year, not to the end, which falls into early 1364, when Longchenpa actually died (see *Kindly Bent to Ease Us*, Part I, p. xv). Longchenpa wrote three 'particular injunctions' (zhal-chems), of which this, the Zhal-chems dri-ma med-pa'i-od, is the first and the most accessible. The last two, the Zhal-chems gnad-kyi me-long and the Zhal-chems mthar-thug gcig-ma, are extremely technical, requiring a lengthy commentary for every word.

Now that I Come to Die presents the essentials of Buddhism in a poetic, lyrical form whose special appeal lies in the uses of striking similes and a beseeching refrain. The tenor of these injunctions is the realization of Being, of which it cannot be said that is or is not, but which as dynamic wholeness makes all differentiations and assertions, positive or negative, possible. In its experience, this wholeness is cognitively meaningful from deep within itself and spreads unlimited as the open sky in its felt immediacy. It is impossible to say that this wholeness has ever come into existence as a thing, but precisely because it is not a thing, it remains infinitely fertile.

Homage to all noble persons endowed with great compassion.
Homage to Him who is the sun,
shining in the wondrous brightness of
what is good and pure,
In the primordial (sky-like) ground of Being;
Displaying various manifestations of His compassion
And looking after living beings by His charismatic actions.[1]

Homage to Him who, after completing
All that was to be done by him, went to Kushinagara,[2]
Truly the most wondrous city,
To teach a lesson to those who believe in everlastingness.

From former time I know the nature of samsara:
Therefore, from one about to leave behind
This body which is transitory and deceptive,
Listen to his admonition which is solely for your benefit:
In worldly things there is no abiding essence.

Although you may hold, in this your life,
To it as true, it will most likely deceive you.
Once you have fully understood that you cannot rely
On that which is impermanent and without essence,
Attend to the real meaning of Being straight away.

Friends do not last forever,
but are rather like guests:
They meet occasionally and quickly go their ways.
Dismiss attachment to your companions
in this magic show,
And attend to the real meaning of Being,
which alone is beneficial.

The wealth and possessions you have amassed
must be left behind.
They are like honey — to be enjoyed
by those who did not gather them.
Now, while you still can,
make arrangements
for your needs on the way hereafter —
The wealth that on you
will confer excellent qualities.

The house you have built is going to collapse;
it is only a temporary abode;
You cannot stay on, but must go.
Dismiss your attachment
and craving for places of excitement —
Resort to solitary places straight away.

Friendship and hostility are like the play of children:
Love and hatred for that which has no value
are a blazing fire.
Avoid squabbles and resentments —
Control your mind straight away.

Deeds, having no essence, resemble a magic show:
Although you involve yourself in them for a while,
ultimately they are fruitless.
Cease troubling about this life, dismiss worldly concerns —
Look for the road to deliverance straight away.

Your bodily existence, a unique occasion and right juncture,[3]
Is like a precious boat:
While you still have the power to steer it
across the ocean of frustrations,
Shun laziness, indolence, and idleness —
Activate the power of strenuous exertion straight away.

The real Guru is like an escort on a dangerous road:
With great devotion, confident of body, speech and mind,
Depend on this guide who protects
against the enemy of samsara —
Revere him and rely on him straight away.

Instruction in the profound
is like the elixir of immortality:
Since it is the best cure for the
disease of emotionality,
Depend on your inner being;
Discover precisely its quality —
Imbibe it and allow it to affect you straight away.

The three trainings,[4] when utterly pure,
Are like the Wish-Fulfilling Gem:
They are the path itself, which here and hereafter
Offers bliss, and ultimately leads to
what is good and pure.
Through them you find real peace
In limpid clearness and consummate perspicacity[5]
(your very Being) —
let them develop straight away.

Learnedness is like a precious lamp:
Dispelling darkness and illuminating
The path toward liberation,
Its beacon of prosperity and bliss
Opens the eye of pristine cognitions[6]—
Let it shine unrestricted straight away.

Proper thoughts are like a skilled goldsmith:
They remove all impositions and doubts
About 'this' and 'that'.
By exercising a discriminating awareness
Born from thinking about what you have heard —
Absorb them within you straight away.

Cultivation (of what you have learned)
Is like the taste of nectar:
Through the cultivation of what has been heard
And thought about, all emotional afflictions are remedied,
The ocean of propositions is crossed,
And the other shore of Being is reached —
In forest groves start contemplative cultivation straight away.

Vision is like the bright sky:
Free from all that is high or low, divided or partial,
Neither wide nor narrow,
It is beyond attempts to verbalize it —
Apply the tool of understanding straight away.

Contemplation is like a mountain or a sea:
Neither moving or changing, it is lucent and unsullied:
All labeling that erupts

Through the proliferation of perturbations thus ceases —
Contemplate (things) as they really are straight away.

Conduct is like the wise person:
It acts in accordance with what is appropriate and beneficial.
This realm of magic with its attachments and clingings,
acceptances and rejections, denials and affirmations —
Free it from the object-subject division straight away.

Fruition is like a guide gathering riches:
Wealthy himself, he allows others' values
spontaneously to come forth.
Without expectations and apprehensions,
the mind feels naturally blissful —
Exert yourself to win this wealth straight away.

Mind, continual source of meanings, is like the sky:
The sky is Mind,[7] genuine meaningfulness,
Without duality, complete and identical with itself —
Understand it thoroughly straight away.

All the variety of things and ideas
are like images in a mirror:
Void of appearances, there is yet no emptiness;

If (this paradox) is left unresolved
As to being identical or different, complacency prevails —
Know the experience thoroughly for what it is straight away.
The subject dealing with its object is like a dream:
Although there is no duality (of subject and object),
Ingrained tendencies cause duality to appear.
What is postulated by the intellect
Is nothing self-sufficient —
Know non-duality straight away.

Mistaken identities are like a
parade of happiness and misery:
Once good and evil
have individually arisen they perpetuate themselves.
In actuality they remain unborn;
in facticity they neither move nor change —
Know this thoroughly straight away.

Intellectual postulates are like the quarrels of foolish men:
There is nothing substantial about them.
Divisive notions have introduced a split and
Philosophical axioms will take
good and evil to be separate —
Know identity straight away.

The bestowing of gifts is like a precious treasure:
Inexhaustible, increasing ever more,
the cause of good fortune.
To the fields of merits,
whether they be inferior, mediocre, or superior[8] —
Give what is deserving straight away.

Self-discipline is like a fine, clean carriage:
The ladder for climbing up to heaven
or to the citadel of happiness.
Restraint, adherence to what is meaningful,
and aiding all beings —
Let these qualities abide in yourself straight away.

Patience is like the unruffled ocean:
It cannot be disturbed by injury;
it is the best rigorous training.
Accepting frustrations and developing
a sense of compassion —
Accustom and familiarize yourself with patience straight away.

Effort is like a blazing bonfire:
Burning away the unsuitable,
it rushes toward the good.

Neither idle, unconcerned, nor lazy —
Realize this path towards deliverance straight away.

Concentration, unswerving, is like the king of mountains:
Unshaken by objectifying tendencies, unperturbed in the presence of objects,
Wherever it is firmly settled,
it cannot be upset by anything —
Familiarize yourself with it straight away.

Appreciation is like the sun's great orb:
Dispelling the darkness of your mind's murkiness
and causing the real meaning to shine,
Raising up the sublime island of deliverance
and drying up the ocean of evil —
Intensify it straight away.

Appropriate action is like a sea captain
In charge of his precious cargo:
With it you cross the ocean of frustration,
Go to the island of utter bliss, and
Realize the three sublime strata
Whereby the twofold aim of like
Is spontaneously fulfilled[9] —
Benefit others by appropriate action straight away.

Strength is like a hero conquering his enemies:
It overcomes the army of emotions
and proceeds toward enlightenment.
Since strength does not admit of hindrances,
and by it wholesomeness will reach its ultimate quality —
Develop it in yourself straight away.

Supplication is like the Wish-fulfilling Gem:
All desires are granted and bliss grows naturally.
It puts the mind at rest and fulfills one's expectations —
Give supplication its great chance straight away.

Pristine awareness is like clouds gathering in the sky:
From the nourishing clouds of holistic feelings,
it lets fall the rain of prosperity and bliss,
and makes the crop of the wholesome
prosper in all beings —
Make efforts to gain this awareness straight away.

Appropriate action and appreciation
are like excellent steeds:
Never stumbling into worldliness or quiescence
one's own and others' values are realized.
The five paths[10] are traversed to their end,

And the three strata are spontaneously present —
Realize these two through your efforts straight away.

Qualities conductive to (the realization of)
Limpid clearness and consummate perspicacity are
like a highway;
The road has been and will be traveled
by noble people throughout all time,
Beginning with the four inspections,
there are thirty-seven qualities in all[11]—
Make effort to develop them straight away.

Kindness is like one's parents
Caring ceaselessly for their children,
the six kinds of beings,[12]
Their love forever aids and enables
(spiritual) success to be realized —
Familiarize yourself with kindness straight away.

Compassion is like the Bodhisattvas,
the Buddha's spiritual sons:
Clothed in the armor of perseverance, they desire to free
Beings from suffering, as if it were their own —
Let compassion grow in yourself straight away.

Joy is like the considerate family elders:
Happy over the welfare of others,
They delight in providing for such welfare —
Attend intensively to joy straight away.

Equanimity is like the level earth:
Without attachment or aversion to those near or far.
and free from afflictions,
Great bliss emerges from its everlasting evenness —
Familiarize yourself with equanimity straight away.

Aspiration and perseverance, needed
for realizing limpid clearness and consummate perspicacity;
are like a true leader:
The helmsman, guiding (you)
to the island of deliverance
where all wholesomeness is found.
Not deterred by worldliness,
The value in others stands out —
Over and over again bring aspiration
And perseverance to life straight away.

Devotion is like the great ocean and high seas:
Full of what is wholesome,
maintaining one flavor throughout.

Its waves of faith surge, never wavering —
Let devotion swell in your heart straight away.

Dedication is like the inexhaustible treasure of the sky:
By dedicating everything to the realm of reality,
Wealth will not lessen
but will grow even more.
(In) the one-flavored stratum of meaningfulness,
the other two strata are spontaneously present —
purify the three aspects (of the situation[13]) —
from their concretization straight away.

Rejoicing is like the value of the sky:
Its merits are unlimited,
it is unobjectifiable and without pride,
Thoroughly transparent and unshakable —
Let rejoicing grow on and on straight away.

Furthermore, inspection is like an iron hook:
It keeps in check the untamed,
drunken elephant of mind.
Turning it away from evil and
tying it to what is wholesome —
Let inspection reside in you straight away.

Circumspect alertness is like an attentive sentinel:
It does not offer the thief, unwholesomeness, a chance;
It is there to guard the wealth of wholesomeness —
Have such alertness with you straight away.

Concern is like the world-encircling mountain:
It is safe from the thieving horde of emotions
And it commands the army that defeats karmic actions —
Make effort to guard the mind straight away.

Trust is like a fertile field:
It lets all desires grow into the harvest
of limpid clearness and consummate perspicacity;
The field of bliss here and hereafter,
trust always yields good fortune —
Let it increase straight away.

Generosity is like a lovely lotus pond:
What is genuine gathers there,
delightful to behold.
It is true enjoyment; it is its own reward —
Let generosity bring joy to others straight away.

Pleasant speech is like the sound of thunder:
It captivates and pleases the minds of beings,
It reverberates around those to be taught

and makes them feel happy —
Gladden others by singing their praises straight away.

Calm behavior is like a true sage:
Unwholesomeness ceases, and
people's trust increases.
Give up artificiality and (follow) natural discipline —
Make this your supreme conduct straight away.

Life's real meaning is like the Buddha's power:
In accord with everything,
yet superior to all;
Similar to everything, yet dissimilar to all —
Let it reside in yourself straight away.

Opportunities are unstable, like autumn clouds:
Their occasion is certain to dissipate;
They have no solid core —
Thoroughly and from your heart
understand this straight away.

All beings are transients, like past and future guests:
The old have gone, the young will also go.
This generation won't even last a hundred years —
Understand this thoroughly straight away.

The presence of this life is like a single day;
The presence of the intermediate state
is like tonight's dream.
The presence of a future life
will come as quickly as tomorrow –
Deal with life's real meaning straight away.

When all that is important has been
illustrated by appropriate examples,
To those who have firm trust, my exhortation is:
What has come together will have to separate.
Hence I shall not tarry,
but will proceed to the island of deliverance.
Since no reliance can be placed on the things of samsara,
Let me sit down firmly on Being's unborn throne.

The appearances in this world are like a trickster:
Mendacious, a wanton whore.
Since they turn the mind from the wholesome
and cause the crowd of emotions to increase,
Send them far away and practice what is right.

Without contentment, even 'wealth' is poverty.
The avaricious mind enjoys no satisfaction.

Contentment itself is the greatest wealth;
Even a little fills the mind with happiness.

Wine and women are the
source of emotional turmoil.
Dismiss such thoughts that cause
clinging, hankering, and craving.
Set out to emulate the sages
And contemplate in sylvan solitudes the
values of inner calm.

With mind focused on the wholesome, day and night,
Renounce wrongdoing and
do what is beneficial,
as the Buddha has advised:
Unswervingly practice what is right.
Then you need not worry about death,
for things will develop as they should.

Through actions and supplications
developed over a long period of time,
Learning and commitment naturally reside
in the disciples who must eventually go their own ways.
So also the teacher and disciple must part —
Know them to be like customers in a marketplace.

These words are spoken from the heart,
for (your) sole benefit:
Give up the distractions and diversions of this life
Which are provided by country, property,
friends, and relatives,
and cultivate meditation in quiet places.

When nothing prevails anymore,
and the time has come to pass on,
You need (to understand the) real meaning (of life),
fearless of death.
Familiarize yourself with the quintessence
of the profoundness of the Guru's instruction.
Make effort (to comprehend it) straight away.

Strive to realize this ultimate bliss,
good through and through,
The very light within,
The mystery of the within in the within,
The most supreme, the path
towards Buddhahood within a single lifetime.

Seek the meaning which worthy men transmit
By possessing the immortality-giving essence,

Being's profound value.
Experience their unique meaning
through the power of your efforts
and quickly reach the citadel of the Victorious One.

Straight away bliss supreme is realized and
Even at a later time benefits accrue.
Strive from now on for the quintessence of Being
With its vast qualities both seen an unseen.

The stars, attendants of the full moon
in a cloudless sky, have assembled.
The Lord of stars himself is about to appear.
The lotus-face of the Lord of Compassion
is made even more beautiful
by the host of Dakas and Dakinis,
With their canopies, umbrellas, royal standards,
and courtly music.
Gently he breathes on me, intimating my acceptance.

The time has come to go; like a traveler,
I must be on my way.
My joy in dying has been well earned: It is
Greater than all the wealth in the ocean

a merchant may have won, or
The godlike power of having conquered armies, or
The bliss found in meditation.
So I, Padma-las-' brel-rtsal[14], wait no longer,
But go to sit firmly on my seat
in the bliss supreme that knows no death.

This life is finished, Karma is exhausted,
What supplication could achieve has ended;
Worldliness is done with; this life's show is over,
Having realized, in one moment.
The very nature of (Being's) self-manifestation
Through the vast realms
in the intermediate state,
I am close to taking up my seat
At the beginning of all and everything.

The riches found in myself have made the
minds of others happy.
Through this magic existence the opulence
of the island of deliverance has been realized.
Having been with you, my excellent disciples,
during this time,
I have been satiated with the joy of meaningfulness.

Now that the connection with this life
has lost its karmic power,
Do not lament about this beggar
who died happily and unattached,
But constantly pray (that he be with you in spirit).

These words spoken for your benefit
Are like a multitude of lotus-flowers
gladdening the bee (-like) trusting beings.

Through the good of these words
May the beings of the three worlds
Go to the place of the origin
of all and everything – nirvana.

The Four Immeasurably Great Catalysts of Being

Equanimity, Love, Compassion, & Joy

translation, introduction, and annotations by
Herbert V. Guenther

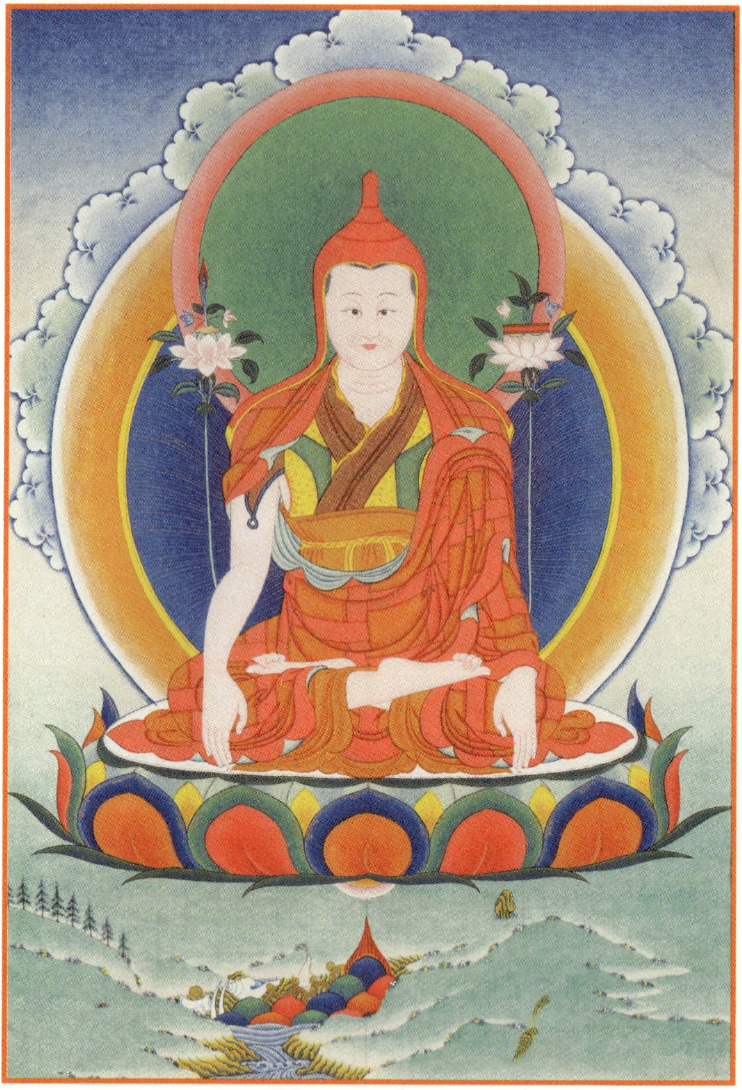

The Four Immeasurably Great Catalysts of Being

Growth remains an individual task that is made possible by (and starts from) inner strength and a feeling of shelteredness. Regardless of whether the growth is induced form outside or comes directly from within, it never occurs in a vacuum or in isolation from other growth-aiding forces. Inner strength, in particular, elicits in us the capacity to reach out towards a deeper and wider dimension in human beings, abolishing the individual's self-imposed loneliness. Inner strength makes us participate, and participation means as much to give ourselves to others as it does to receive others into ourselves. This participation occurs through four fundamental properties, which are equally agents, sensibilities, perceptibilities, and feelings: love, compassion, joyfulness, and equanimity, all of these suggesting and implying thoughtfulness for another's welfare, well-being, success, serenity or the like, when taken in their positive connotation. Negatively, they are mere sentimental impulses inducing euphoric states in a make-believe world that is detrimental to growth.

It is in their positive aspect as honest feelings that these four feelings aid our growth. There exists an intimate interrelationship of balancing and of effects and counterfeits amongst the four feelings. Love may turn into an inordinate clinging to the love-'object'. This becomes a source of frustration that can be countered by compassion as the active force in the removal of suffering. But compassion can turn into sentimentality and a feeling of helplessness — there is so much suffering and whatever is done about it is of no avail.

This feeling can be countered by joyfulness as the affirmation of fulfillment — that which had to be done and the other's development is as much a source of joy as is my own. But joyfulness may turn into a feeling of elation which with its overexcitement makes a person lose himself in unreal goals to which he becomes inordinately attached. It is equanimity that can bring the person back to solid ground, but when equanimity becomes mere apathy and passivity, love with its desire for the other's happiness and welfare acts as a potent counteragent.

Thus a man who by having taken refuge has become the site for spiritual growth
Will cultivate his mind for the welfare of those who are alive
By letting the flower of compassion
blossom in the soil of love
And tending it with the pure water of equanimity
in the cool shade of joyfulness.

As long as these four cardinal agents are not linked to
the road to deliverance,
They are but euphoric states and remain
the cause of fictitious being.
But if the way to inner peace has taken hold of them,
They are the four immeasurably great properties of real
Being because they make us cross the ocean of
fictitious being.

They have as their objective reference the countless
living beings as well as the absolutely real; while
Their own observable quality is, in an all-encompassing
way, referential or non-referential.

In the former case they are related to
a strictly limited number of living beings,

and their (corresponding) observable mental attitudes
being impure, they are referential and
the cause of euphoric states.

They are non-referential when they operate in the
direction of deliverance
And they will be mastered by those who are
compassion themselves.

Those who are unhappy or tormented by frustrations,
Or engrossed in their happiness and wealth, or who are
deeply attached to or bitterly set against anyone,
be they near or far,
Are the objects for love, compassion,
joyfulness, and equanimity.

Their (corresponding) observable mental attitudes are
the desire that there be happiness and that there be
freedom from suffering,
That there be no separation from joyfulness, and that
the mind may operate in calmness.

Although there is no fixed order in their practice,
The beginner should at first develop equanimity.

When he has become impassive about those near and
far he may then develop the other three properties.

As the objective reference is all sentient beings,
You should examine your mind in this way:
"To be attached to father and mother and friends
And to hate an enemy would be a bad attitude.

In the cycle of existence that has neither
beginning nor end, even this my enemy
Has once been my father or mother and
has added to my prosperity.
Can I harbor malice to repay his kindness?"

"Even this my friend here has been my enemy and
has done me harm;
And even now I am subject to the misery he has brought about.
How could it be reasonable to pay him back in his own coin?
Even neutral persons have been friends or enemies.
As there is no certainty as to prosperity or harm,
attachment and hatred are unreasonable."

Therefore, first you must give up attachment to
those who are your friends,

And you must treat them as neutral.
Then you must give up being hateful of your enemies
and must treat them, too, as neutral, annulling the
distinction between those near and those far away.

In order to be rid of the mental darkness
(that still exists in dealing with others as) neutrals,
Cultivate a mind that abolishes the emotions that will
make you again see beings as friends or foes,
And let it be free from fictions about the world.

Just have the sole desire, as have all others,
to be happy and to be rid of misery.
Otherwise, in your ignorance, you will lay the
foundation for suffering.

"Ah! Would that the emotions of beings
who are worn out by them,
Together with all their latent tendencies,
come to rest, and mind calm down.
Would that all embodied beings tormented by the
violence of attachment and hatred
Calm down in mind so that
it no longer oscillates between those

near and those far away, and is free
from attachment and hatred."

Thinking in this way, move on in contemplation from
one being to two, to three,
To one country, to one continent,
to the four continents, and
From one, two, three thousand worlds to all worlds.
The measure of this cultivation is to see yourself and others,
friends and enemies, as being alike.

Afterwards you can move on to non-referential equanimity;
Everything is mind and this being Mind-as-such is like
the spacious sky.
Let your mind, free from all propositions about it,
Settle in this sphere that in the ultimate sense has never
come into existence and is utterly open.

The measure of this cultivation is the birth of a
profound and calm understanding.

The result is that mind without the
mire of nearness and distance
Is the spontaneous presence of ultimacy.

When thus the mind has become calm in every aspect,
Think of all embodied beings in the same manner
As you yourself would like your mother to be happy.

The objective reference of love is all sentient beings and
Its observable quality is a mind that intends to let them,
temporarily, find the happiness of gods and men
And, ultimately, to realize limpid clearness and
consummate perspicacity[15].
Cultivate love by moving in thought from one person to
all beings, to the very limits of the ten directions.

The indication (of its cultivation) is a
supreme, all-encompassing love
Greater than the love a mother has for her only child.

Afterwards to have everything in this
reach and range of sameness
Is the great, non-referential love.

Its indication is the unity of love and openness of Being.
The result is, visibly, pure pleasantness and nobleness.
Immediately after you have engulfed living beings in love,
You should develop compassion

by thinking of their suffering
In the same way as you are unable to bear mentally the
suffering of your parents:

"How wearied are my parents, having done so much for me,
By various frustrations;
They have committed evil for my sake and
Are now tormented by heat and cold,
hunger and thirst, and executions;
They drown in the turbulent sea of birth, old age,
sickness, and death.

How pitiable are they, drifting about in endless Samsara,
Desirous to be delivered from it
but with no peace of mind,
There being no friendly helpers
to show them the right way.
Could I, having seen them, possibly cast them away?"

You should think deep in your heart and marrow:
"Might all beings be delivered in a moment
From suffering through the good (accumulated by me
over) the three aspects of time,
And through my bodily existence and my wealth."

The inability to bear the suffering of living beings is
said to be the indication (of compassion).

The indication of having, through a non-referential
compassion, entered a state of composure that
extends into its subsequent state,
Is the unity of the openness of Being and compassion.

The result is a mind without malice and vindictiveness
In all its fitness and primordial purity.

Then when each living being is happy
By being soaked with compassion,
you should cultivate joyfulness.

The objective reference is all sentient beings
And you should cultivate joyfulness in thinking:
"Ah, there is no need for me to install
All these beings in happiness;
Each of them having found his happiness,
Might they from now onwards, until they are pervaded
by limpid clearness and consummate perspicacity,
Never be separated from
this pleasure and happiness."

The indication is the birth of joy without envy.
Thereafter comes a joyfulness (as) in pure concentration.
Body, speech, and mind are spontaneously calm and happy.
The result is steadfastness and joyfulness
through this inner wealth.

After you have become accustomed to this you should
cultivate an order, beginning with love;
Thereby addiction to these four immeasurably great
properties is gradually stopped.

When, through the cultivation of love, you become
attached to everyone as your friend, it is
Through compassion that involvement in the cause and
effect relationship of suffering is ended.

When, through an inferior compassion,
you stay with the objective reference,
It is through a non-referential joyfulness
that weariness is ended.

When, through joyfulness,
the mind is agitated and becomes overexcited,
You must cultivate equanimity which is free from

attachment to those near and far.
When equanimity is (passively) neutral and indeterminate,
You have, as before, to cultivate love
and the other immeasurably great properties.
Thereby the cultivation (of these immeasurably great
properties) becomes easy and steady.

A practitioner in whom this procedure
has become a steady way
May then cultivate the immeasurably great properties
in their order, outside their order, in a mixed order,
or in leaps and bounds.

Thereby understanding gains freshness
And its steadiness becomes ever more firm.

From among the four results of such cultivation
Maturation is the realization of higher forms of life and
the ultimate good.
In the world of sensuousness you find existence as a
god or man and bring about prosperity and happiness.

The result of compatibility with the cause is that you
cannot act but in this way,

And in its experience you feel a happiness that is
free from anything that might upset it.

The dominant effect is that you are born in a pleasant,
happy, and joyful country,
That people are friendly and that you are
resplendent with wealth.

The over-all effect is that the four immeasurably great
properties grow ever more and spread ever farther.
And the bitendential value of Being
is spontaneously fulfilled.

When love is present and acting on hatred,
there comes in its place
A pristine cognition that is like a mirror, and the
founding stratum of meaningful engagement is present.
This founding stratum of meaningful engagement is
adorned with the major and minor marks of Buddhahood.

When compassion is present and acting on cupidity,
there comes in its place
A pristine cognition that is individualizing, and its
founding stratum of meaning.

This founding stratum is the distinct Buddha-qualities
such as his powers and so on.

When joyfulness is present and acting on envy,
there comes in its place
A pristine cognition that knows things to be
as they should be, and its founding
stratum of embodiment of meaning.
This founding stratum is not something fixed, but
comes in various forms:
Their spontaneous embodiments are its charismatic activity.

When equanimity is present and acting on arrogance
and darkness, there comes in their place
The two pristine cognitions of the equality (of all that is) and
of the meaningfulness-continuum, and the
'founding stratum of the facticity of Being'.
This founding stratum is the meaningfulness
(of experience) defying any propositions about it[16].

Thus the teacher of gods and men has praised
love and the other agents
As having vast qualities and being without compare.
A path that does not have them is a wrong path;

Taking refuge in other teachers is an evil path;
But a path that has them is the highway
That the previous and future Buddhas through all
three aspects of time have traveled and
will travel towards spotless deliverance.

When it is claimed by the cause-dominated pursuit
that, like a seed producing its sprouts,
Appropriate action and appreciative discrimination
set up the two founding strata[17],
While by the goal-sustained pursuit both are
acknowledged as the necessary conditions that remove
The two obscurations[18] of the founding strata,
They are actually saying the same, since appropriate
action in itself depends upon the path delineated by
immeasurable compassion;
Both the cause-dominated and goal-sustained pursuits
experience alike the openness of Being as having the
character of compassion.

Furthermore, it has been said in the Sutras that
since beginningless time
The absolutely positive has been there from the very
beginning as a seed uncreated.

With this statement the Tantras agree, claiming to burn away the obscurations
That have, incidentally, from the very beginning veiled the three founding strata.
In brief, sages and saints have spoken of an
outer and inner aspect
Of the common goal of the Sutra and Tantra paths.
Therefore, emulating the worthy Buddha-sons,
Make decisive efforts to practice the
four immeasurably great properties.

When by this well-explained inner peace
The mire of mind in all living beings has cleared,
May Mind, wearied and weakened by its
Pursuit of wrong ways and its descending to low levels,
Today find comfort and ease.

Longchenpa's Verses and Commentary on the Immeasurably Great Catalysts of Being

Equanimity, Love, Compassion, & Joy

translation by the
Yeshe De Translation Group

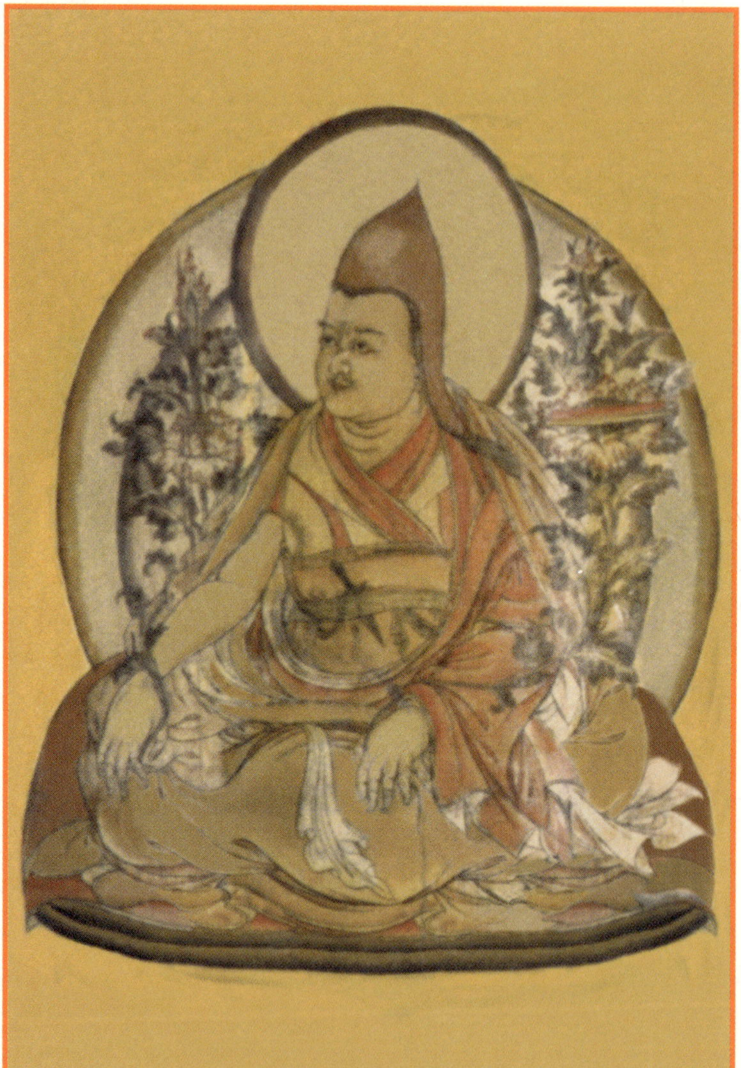

Longchenpa's Verses and Commentary on the Immeasurably Great Catalysts of Being

Part One — Contemplating Equanimity

1 NECESSITY FOR CONTEMPLATING EQUANIMITY

There is no single way way of contemplating equanimity that is all-inclusive.

> *Although there is no specific order for their practice,*
> *beginners should start with equanimity.*
> *When you have become impartial*
> *towards those close to you and those distant,*
> *then practice the other three Immeasurables.*

It is taught that practice should begin with what is easiest to produce in your mind stream. However, until you become impartial towards those close to you and those distant, it will be difficult for the other three Immeasurables to arise. Therefore, the beginner should start with equanimity.

The master Yeshe Nyingpo (Jnanagarba) states in the dBu-ma-rgyan: "On the well-prepared ground of equanimity, the flowers of love are scattered. They are embellished with the shade of compassion and purified by the clear waters of joy."

The rTag-gnyis states: "At first you should meditate on love, secondly on compassion, thirdly meditate on joy, and last of all, on equanimity." This instruction is for those under the direction of teachers who are applying themselves to the thatness (tattva) of the inner deity. For them, it is easier at the beginning to produce the nature of love, compassion, and joy.

2   THE OBJECTIVE FOCUS OF MEDITATION ON EQUANIMITY:

Since the objective focus is all living beings,
examine your own states of mind in this way:
Attachment to your present father and mother and friends
and hatred toward enemies — states like that are bad for you.

Since each and every sentient being has been in the past both friend and enemy, to feel attachment or hatred for them makes no sense.

3   EQUANIMITY, KEEPING IN MIND THE KINDNESS OF OTHERS:

While wandering in samsara throughout
beginningless and endless time
even my enemy has been my father and mother,
befriended me, and brought about my benefit
How could I return this kindness with malice?

How can it be right to return harm for previous help? In the Vinaya it states: "In return for benefit, benefit is the best response. It cannot be right to respond with harm or even with neutrality."

4 Equanimity, contemplating the uncertainty of friends and enemies

Throughout many lifetimes,
even this my friend has been my enemy and brought me harm.
Even now, I suffer from that harm.
How could it be right to return such harm with help?
Even those toward whom I am indifferent
have been my friends and enemies.
Help and harm are hard to ascertain,
so hatred and attachment are never right.

From the Twenty-five Thousand Line Prajnaparamita: "Subhuti, you should contemplate equality and mutual benefit toward all sentient beings, generating the mind of equanimity."

5 Equanimity, contemplating sameness

Therefore, first, abandon attachment toward
loved ones and friends, treating them as neutrals.

Then, abandoning hatred toward enemies
and treating them as neutrals as well,
be without bias toward those close or distant.

When you are impartial to both friend and enemy,

6   MEDITATE ON EQUANIMITY, FOR THE SAKE OF BENEFITING ALL BEINGS:

In order to be free from the obscuring aspects of disinterest,
impartially clear away the emotionality of sentient beings,
and meditate as if you all were free from samsara.

Because even the disinterested mind is obscured, after working with that, pacify the emotionality of all sentient beings influenced by enmity and friendship. May no form of attachment or hatred arise! May each of us mutually gain mastery over mind.

7   EQUANIMITY, CONTEMPLATING UNIVERSAL FREEDOM FROM SUFFERING:

Everyone is alike in wishing for happiness
and wishing to rid themselves of pain.
Yet in ignorance, they create the causes of suffering.

All sentient beings are alike in rejoicing at happiness while not wanting to suffer. Since this is so, how can it be right to think of harming others? Although we desire happiness, our actions are involved with nonvirtue, the cause of suffering. We must reverse this!

8   THE ACTUAL FOCUS OF EQUANIMITY:

Alas, the emotional torment of beings! May I develop
the mind of equanimity so as to calm
the emotions of beings together with their underlying tendencies.
May all beings who are tormented by fierce hatred and attachment
toward those near and far
become impartial, free from hatred and attachment.

In such a way, may all the emotionality of beings be calmed. In particular, after having calmed the raging fires of desire and hatred, develop mastery of mind so that you are impartial to those both close and distant.

9   EXPANDING THE FOCUS OF THE MIND OF EQUANIMITY:

Thinking in such a way, meditate on one being,
then two, and then three;
meditate on one country, then one continent,

then four continents;
meditate on a thousand worlds, then two thousand, and
then three; then meditate on the whole universe.

The beginner meditates on what has not yet been purified with respect to personal friends and enemies. Then the beginner meditates on one, two, three, and more sentient beings, up to his or her own city, country, and then all the countries of the world and beyond. After that, meditate, starting with the continent of Lus-´phags, up to a whole world-system, then one thousand, two, and three thousand worlds. Also, in the same way one should meditate first on sameness of all human beings, and then on that of all animals and so on, up to all six classes of beings.

10 MEASURING THE CULTIVATION OF EQUANIMITY IN YOUR STREAM OF CONSCIOUSNESS:

The measure of its cultivation is the degree of
sameness of self and other, friend and foe.
Once such a mind is gained, complete impartiality emerges
in which anger or jealousy are never produced toward anyone at all.

11 THE POST-ATTAINMENT OF CONTEMPLATING EQUANIMITY, AFTER YOU HAVE MEDITATED WITH A FOCUS:

Afterwards, the object of equanimity is without a focus:
All is mind; the mind itself is like the sky.
In that sphere of openness, the Ultimate, unproduced,
one becomes settled in freedom from mental reflection and projection.

Review:

Again, the object of meditation appears in the form of sentient beings, although one becomes settled in the sphere of remembering that: "such beings, like reflections, actually do not exist; they appear, but are unproduced by their very nature." Moreover, taking the skandhas as objective realities, and then from that, because of holding to "self", there is attachment to "other." But both self and other have the nature of falsehood, like imagining the reflection on the mirror is one's face. Like such imaginings, while not existing, they do appear, depending on the skandhas.

From the Rin-chen-phreng-ba:

Just as in dependence upon a mirror,
A reflection of oneself or another appears,
in reality, self and other do not in the slightest exist in the mirror.
In the same way, in dependence on the skandhas,
holding to the 'I' becomes your reference point.
And yet, like the reflection of one's face,
there is nothing there at all that is real.

Without the support of a mirror,
A reflection of one's face does not appear.
In the same way, without the support of the skandhas,
There is no holding onto an "I".

If you think that the skandhas have a self-nature, if the grasping at a self exists, then karma exists. Since from karma, birth exists, then there exists everything up to old age and death. But with no grasping at the skandhas, all is reversed.

From the Rin-chen-phreng-ba:

So long as holding to the skandhas exists,
There is, from that, the holding to the "I"
If holding to the "I" exists, there is also karma,
From that, then, there is birth.
The three actions without beginning, middle, or end —
each a cause for the other — create the wheel of samsara,
like a circle of light from a spinning torch.
That being so, you don't get anything other than
duality of self and other and the three times of
past, present, and future.

But if the holding to an I is exhausted,
then because of that, karma and birth will be exhausted as well.
Accordingly, when one sees that cause and effect

and birth are exhausted,

one does not regard the world as genuinely existing or not existing.

Therefore, understand that all things are like reflections, there being no objects to grasp as "I" and "mine".

12   THE BENEFITS OF HAVING MEDITATED ON EQUANIMITY:

The measure of this cultivation is the arising of
a realization of profound peace.

There arises the realization of sameness — in that the self-nature of all things is, from the 'beginning' unproduced. In the Kun-byed it says: "By settling free from duality in awakened being (chos-nyid, dharmata) beyond thought, awareness (ye-shes) rises.

13   THE FRUIT OF EQUANIMITY:

The fruit is a mind unsullied by closeness or distance:
the spontaneous nature of the way things truly are.

While in a relative sense, there is no closeness or distance, no self or other, in the absolute sense, there is a realization of being itself (chos-nyid) without duality. Having become well-accustomed to meditating like this, then one should meditate on pure love.

Part Two — Contemplating Love

1 Increasing love

In the manner explained above:

> *When your mind has become impartial towards everyone,*
> *consider all embodied beings in the way*
> *you would long for happiness of your own mother.*

Then, in this state of equanimity, just as we love and delight in our father and mother, the mind settles in an attitude that regards all sentient beings as father and mother, initiating meditation on love.

The Khri-brgyad-stong-pa states: "You should meditate with a mind absorbed in love, never captivated by any of the ways of the Shravaka or Pratyekabuddha."

2 The object of love

What is the object?

> *The object of love is sentient beings —*
> *and with the thought: "May they temporarily meet*
> *with the happiness of gods and humans*

and ultimately meet with the bliss of enlightenment!"
cultivate that love —
starting with one being and continuing to all beings
in every direction to the ends of space.

When seeing sentient beings who are without happiness, one should think: "May they meet with, in the present, the happiness of gods and humans, and ultimately the happiness of a Buddha," and meditate thus upon all living beings, starting from one and continuing up to as many beings as would fill the far reaches of space.

The Yum-bar-ma states: "When you see sentient beings who are without happiness, set your intention on the wish: "May these sentient beings obtain the complete happiness of the gods in the god-realms."

3   THE SIGN OF HAVING CULTIVATED THE MEDITATION ON LOVE:
The cultivation:

The sign of it is a superior love that embraces all,
surpassing the love of a mother for her only child.

Further, seeing any sentient being whatsoever brings forth a feeling of delight and a deep love that draws forth the wish to be of benefit.

4 Love Without an Objective Focus

After meditating on love with an objective focus:

> *Afterwards, all settles into a state of universal sameness —*
> *This is the great love which has no objective focus*
> *Its sign is the coming together of love and emptiness.*

Sentient beings are the object of the meditation on love. One meditates while thinking: "These beings are born from the assembling of the six elements of earth, water, fire, space, wind, and consciousness. Whether analyzed coarsely, as atoms, or subtly, according to real meaning and pure consciousness, they have no substantial existence and are thus like space." According to the Rin-chen-phreng-ba:

> *Beings are not earth, not water,*
> *not fire, not wind, not space,*
> *not consciousness, not all of these altogether;*
> *yet what being could be other than these?*
> *Because beings are composed of the six elements,*
> *they are not real; and in the same way*
> *each of the elements, in being compounded, is not real.*
> *The skandhas are not the self, and the self is not in them.*
> *The self is not that, nor is it absent from that.*

Continuing, the text relates:

When one can find no substance,
how can there be absence of substance?
Because it is nothing but an absence of form,
space is also nothing but a name.
If there is no arising, how can there be form?
Therefore, it does not exist even as a name.
In the same way as arising and the self are considered,
so one should consider feeling, perception, motivation
and consciousness — therefore the six elements are without a self.

In what way are they non-existent? If one analyzes the elements of the body that appear as a sentient being, they do not exist either. Since a consciousness that supports them or is supported by them is not seen, they do not become objectified as a self or what belongs to the self. When investigating and analyzing in such way, one sees they are, in essence, empty. The same text also states:

Just as if the fronds of a plantain tree
were completely removed,
there would be nothing left at all ,
in the same way if the elements making up a living being
were destroyed, there would be nothing there.
Thus, it was said by the Jinas:
"All things are without a self."

Further, what appears to us in our sight or hearing is neither true nor false: Truth and falsity are things that the mind arranges. The same text states: "Seeing, hearing, and the like are said by the Muni to be neither true nor false." Further in the same text, "This world is beyond truth and falsity."

Truly all things are beyond truth and falsity, like the plantain tree. The Ting-nge-dzin-rgyal-po also speaks of this:

> *This false trunk of a plantain tree ;*
> *when cut open by someone looking for the core,*
> *turns out to have no core, inside or out.*
> *Know all things to be the same.*

The sign of cultivation is the arising of love and at the same time the realization that the essence of beings is, like the plantain tree, devoid of a self-nature or self.

5   THE FRUIT OF MEDITATING ON LOVE:
What is the fruit?

The fruit is to attain pure delight in what is seen.

Further, all sentient beings are delighted when they see you and you are delighted by all you see, thus is accomplished the purification of the turbidity of attachment, hatred, and so forth. The brGyad-stong-pa states:

Through having meditated many times with a mind of love and having stabilized this meditation, when one sees beings there is delight and never anger.

Also, with regard to acquiring immeasurable merit, the Thar-pa-chen-po-phyogs-rgyas-pa-i-mdo states:

> *Compared to someone in pure worlds,*
> *who for an entire kalpa*
> *maintains pure morality,*
> *the merit of the being who, for just an instant of joy,*
> *practices love, is far greater.*
>
> *Anyone who, in this worldly realm,*
> *has committed sins of body, speech, and mind,*
> *though they are certain to fall into the lower realms,*
> *through such love can be cleansed in an instant.*

Part Three — Contemplating Compassion

1   BRINGING TO MIND THE SUFFERING OF BEINGS:
Now, compassion will be taught.

After surrounding all beings in love,
compassion is generated
when the suffering of beings is brought to mind —
in the same way that your mind cannot bear
the suffering of your father and mother.

Concentrating, one thinks: "My kind fathers and mothers, through the sins that they have done for my sake, are now tormented by suffering in the three lower realms and the like. They are so greatly to be pitied! I must extricate them!" Thus in the Yum-bar-ma it states:

When seeing suffering sentient beings, in thinking about them, there comes to mind the thought: "May these sentient beings freed from suffering!"

2   THE WAY TO MEDITATE ON COMPASSION:
As to how to meditate:

My fathers and mothers who have shown such great kindness to me
through having committed sins for my sake,
are tormented by heat, cold, thirst, and being killed.
Sunk in the vast turbulent river of birth, old age, sickness, and death,
they are afflicted by every kind of suffering!

3   Explanation of the Substance of Compassion

In this continual suffering:

The tranquil mind that desires release from suffering is absent,
as are spiritual friends to show them the true path. Therefore, alas,
they wander pitifully in samsara without end.
Seeing all this, how could one bear to abandon them?

One must consider: "Sentient beings who wander like this undergo great suffering; they do not even know there is a way to escape. Even spiritual friends of virtue are not able to show the path of liberation to them all; only to a few. Yet of those who are now endlessly circling and suffering, there is not one who in former times has not been my father, mother, and friend; if I were to abandon these same beings who are without protector or refuge, it would be like abandoning my mother and father."

In the Slob-spring (Shishyalekha, 98) is states:

Who could forsake these
suffering, unprotected beings, these fettered ones
when, in the past, they sheltered us and took us into their hearts,
with a mind of caring and love.

4   EXPLANATION OF THE CIRCUMSTANCES FOR GENERATING COMPASSION:

The circumstances are:

Therefore, from the depths of your heart and the marrow of your bones,
you must think: "Through my body, possessions,
and virtuous action of past, present, and future,
may the sufferings of beings be instantly removed!"

In this way, one must think from deep within the heart: "May the transference of all my happiness and virtue to other beings remove their suffering, so that they will always have immeasurable happiness!" The Khri-brgyad-stong-pa states: "One must meditate on the broad and noble mind endowed with great compassion and not on the way of the common path of the Shravakas and Pratyekabuddhas."

5   EXPLANATION OF THE SIGN OF HAVING CULTIVATED COMPASSION:

When compassion has been cultivated through this meditation, starting with one sentient being and continuing to all:

*The inability to bear the suffering of
sentient beings is the sign.*

The suffering of even those most distant becomes even harder to bear than one's own pain.

6   EXPLANATION OF THE MEDITATION AND POST-MEDITATION ON COMPASSION:

Alternate sessions of meditation on compassion with an object, and then expand it towards "everything":

*Through compassion that has no object,
one settles afterwards in a state of equipoise:
Its sign is that compassion is conjoined with shunyata.*

One must then think: "Truly the objects of compassion, sentient beings, if analyzed and investigated, do not exist by their own nature; their appearance is like a mirage, in which water appears where is none!

The Ting-nge-dzin-rgyal-po states:

*Just as at noon on a summer day
beings who travel, tormented by thirst,
see the mirage of mass of water,
know all things to be just the same.*

And the Rin-chen-phreng-ba states:

> *Just as a mirage resembles water*
> *but is not water and is not real,*
> *so the skandhas resemble a self*
> *but are not a self and are not real.*
>
> *Someone who has advanced toward a mirage*
> *thinking: "there is water there!"*
> *once finding nothing there,*
> *would be stupid to grasp at it.*
>
> *In the same way,*
> *the world does not exist —*
> *being just like a mirage.*
> *To say: "It exists"*
> *and grasp at it is deluded indeed.*
> *If this delusion "exists"*
> *there is no escape.*

Further in the same text it states:

> *Because neither of them in reality*
> *come or go or stay,*
> *this world is nirvana.*

And later it states:

*For that reason, the Buddhas
explain the immortal doctrine as profound
going beyond being and non-being.*

Through meditating in this way, having deeply understood the nature of all things, emptiness and compassion are united. This is the practice of the sacred path. If either one of these is missing, the path is mistaken. In the Doha-mdzod it states:

*Whoever enters into emptiness devoid of compassion
does not obtain the superior path.
Someone who meditates on compassion alone
will remain in samsara, unliberated.
Those who are able to join the two together
will dwell neither in samsara or nirvana.*

7 THE RESULT OF MEDITATION ON COMPASSION

Meditating in that way:

*The result is a mind
freed from malice and violence,
dynamic and in a state of original purity.*

There is the attainment of a dynamic mind free from malice and violence, as well as the accomplishment of the enlightenment of a Buddha.

In the sNying-po-mchog it states:

*Through great compassion one obtains
a dynamic mind, non-violence,
and supreme accomplishment adorned with joy.*

Part Four — Contemplating Joy

1 **THE NECESSITY OF CONTEMPLATING JOY:**
Now, joy will be explained. In the manner just explained:

> *Towards the samsaric travelers who have*
> *thus been bathed in compassion,*
> *meditate joyfully:*
> *"May each dwell in happiness."*

Thus, when one sees a happy sentient being, one meditates on joy. In the Nyi-khri it states: "When one sees any sentient being endowed with individual happiness, one thinks like this: "May this person never be separated from this happiness! May this person pass beyond the happiness of gods and humans and obtain all-knowing happiness!"

2 **EXPLANATION OF THE OBJECTIVE FOCUS OF THE MEDITATION ON JOY:**
The manner of proceeding:

> *The objective focus is sentient beings who possess happiness.*
> *It takes form in the thought: "Ah, all these samsaric travelers!*

Without any need for me to establish them in happiness,
each has gained happiness, better than I could gain for them.
From now until they have obtained the heart of enlightenment,
may they never be separated from this happiness and joy!"
Beginning with a single being, one extends the meditation to all.

In this way, one meditates on the possession of happiness starting from one sentient being and continuing onward up to everyone.

3 THE MEASURE OF HAVING CULTIVATED JOY:

The measure of having cultivated joy is:

The sign is the birth of joy and the absence of jealousy.

It is the birth of the supreme joy in which there is no jealousy of what others possess.

4 EXPLANATION OF THE ESSENCE OF JOY:

After a period of meditating on joy that has an objective focus:

After that, an unobjectified contemplation is joy itself.

One meditates on the object of joy, all sentient beings, as appearing like an illusion, and having no real existence. The Ting-nge-'dzin-rgyal-po states:

*In the same way that in the midst of a crowd of people
the illusionist manifest various forms
such as horses and oxen and chariots —
that appear to exist although they do not —
know that all things are the same.*

In the Rin-chen-phreng-ba it states:

*It is just what is hidden from ordinary beings
that is profound Dharma.
That the world is like an illusion
is the nectar of the Buddha's teachings.*

*Just as with regard to an illusory elephant
there appears to be coming into being and destruction,
while in reality there is no coming into being and no destruction.*

*In the same way, with regards to the world that is like an illusion,
both coming into being and destruction appear,
but in reality, coming into being and destruction
are non-existent.*

*Just as an illusory elephant
that has come from nowhere and is going nowhere
is therefore nothing more than a delusion of the mind
and in reality does not abide,*

Just so, the illusion-like world
has come from nowhere and is going nowhere,
and because it is nothing more than a delusion of the mind,
in reality it also does not abide.

Thus, someone misconceives that which is mere convention
as bring a true self transcending past, present, and future;
but in a world that both exists and does not exists,
how can anything exist?

5   EXPLANATION OF THE GOOD QUALITIES OF JOY:
Through meditating like that, through the joy of the way things are:

Body, speech, and mind, will be spontaneously
peaceful and happy.

This is the measure.

6   ON THE RESULT OF MEDITATING ON JOY:
The result is that through such application, constant joy will be achieved.

Further, in the brGyad-stong-pa it states: "Whoever possesses the immeasurably broad mind of joy, which no Shravaka or Pratyekabuddha is able to appropriate, will achieve the very highest, perfectly complete state of paradise."

Contemplating Equanimity, Love, Compassion, and Joy Together

Now comes a further explanation of this mode of meditation:

> *After attuning yourself in such a way,*
> *and then progressively meditating,*
> *beginning with love, you will*
> *gradually halt fixation on any of the four.*

If your meditation proceeds as previously suggested, gradually, in stages the antidotes that create liberation are activated.

1   THE GENERAL ANTIDOTES ARE AS FOLLOWS:

Any drawbacks of love are halted by way of meditation on compassion. Thus:

> *If when meditating on love,*
> *you become attached to all beings as if*
> *they were your friends,*
> *through compassion you cease being attracted*
> *to these causes and conditions of suffering.*

Some people develop a constant attachment to others similar to the strong attachment of parents. By meditating on both aspects of compassion, an antidote is formed.

Any drawbacks of compassion are halted by joy. Thus:

If, through a lower form of compassion,
you are caught up in the object of focus,
you halt completely any despair
through unobjectified joy.

If you become attached to a specifically characterized aspect of compassion, you can clear away all ensuing attachment and despair through unobjectified joy, seeing all as an illusion.

Any drawbacks of joy are halted by equanimity. Thus:

When, through joy, the mind becomes addicted
to mental proliferation and agitation,
meditate on great equanimity, free
from attachment to those near and distant.

If you become attached to the joy gained through delighting in the happiness of others, you can clear this away through the meditation on equanimity that is sober and without objective focus. Any drawbacks to equanimity are halted by love. Thus:

If your state of equanimity is
passive and indeterminate,

meditate, progressively as before,
on love and the rest. In such a way,
you will obtain stability and ease
in your practice.

Once you have come to have neutral feelings for everyone, start your meditations again, beginning with love.

While these are the general antidotes, the specific antidote for being caught up in any sort of self-contained objective focus is to meditate without objective focus on each of these as indicated. By meditating in such a way, through purifying your consciousness with relation to each of the Four Immeasurables, you will quickly obtain stability.

2   EXPLANATION ON THE WAY OF MEDITATION ALTERNATELY:

A practitioner who is very stable
in meditation meditates in order,
out of order, alternately, and by leaps.

Having steadied the Four Immeasurables, to enhance them, meditate again in order, beginning with love. Then meditate out of order, backwards, beginning with equanimity. Again meditate alternately on love and joy, on compassion and equanimity; then after meditating on equanimity, meditate on love. With love tuned down, meditate with middling intensity on joy; after meditating on equanimity, meditate with great intensity on love. Establish this pattern until your meditation progresses in an upward spiral in leaps and bounds.

The Yum-bar-ma states:

Subhuti, meditate on love
in such a way.
Meditate on joy.
With respect to compassion,
establish equanimity.
There will then be what is called
'taking up equanimity', and the rest.

3 EXPLANATION OF THE QUALITIES OF MEDITATION: WHY DO YOU NEED TO DO THIS? AND WHAT IS THE WAY?

By these practices, the freshness of
realization is enhanced;
by developing steadfastness,
the support of realization increases.

You obtain the specific freshness of the mind of the Four Immeasurables; unsteadiness is stabilized, then becomes increasingly steady, extremely steady.

4   EXPLANATION OF THE RESULT.

Now, the results of meditating on the Four Immeasurables are presented. The circumstances surrounding these results are explained thus:

> *From the four results of meditating in this way,*
> *the maturation builds up to*
> *both exalted higher states of being and ultimate good (enlightenment);*
> *As for the joy and benefits of obtaining a life as human or god in the desire realm,*

Having attained the form of a god or a human, you exist in an exalted state of being that accomplishes the two accumulations of merit and wisdom, you benefit sentient beings, you are never apart from the Four Immeasurables, and even occasions of carelessness and lethargy or strong pain cannot alienate you from them.

The mDo-sde-rgyan (Sutralamkara) states:

> *Those born in the Desire Realm*
> *abiding in a state of purity*
> *are always wise.*
> *They amass the two accumulations*
> *of merit and wisdom,*
> *and thoroughly mature other sentient beings.*

> *Never apart from complete purity,*
>
> *they are free from whatever is not in accord with purity;*
>
> *even having been careless, and even if the cause of that carelessness*
>
> *has not been exhausted, the wrongdoing does not mature.*

The final result is that they achieve enlightenment. The same text goes on to state:

> *Forsaking harm is the seed of enlightenment.*
>
> *It is the cause of desiring to take up*
>
> *the suffering of others and to create happiness.*
>
> *The actual maturation becomes steadiness in the Dharma:*
>
> *for those children of the Conqueror*
>
> *enlightenment is not far distant.*

Thus, the result of separation from suffering is brought about by forsaking all harm. The dominant result is brought about by activating the seeds of liberation. The enabling result is brought about by patiently enduring suffering as you perform difficult actions in order to make others happy. The result of the concordant cause is brought about by cultivating these four things in this lifetime, whereby you obtain the maturation of these four even in future lifetimes.

For the sons and daughters of the Conqueror, these Four Immeasurables always arise naturally, from meditation, from seeing objects of compassion, and from the diminishing of whatever is inharmonious with the Immeasurables.

In the same text it states:

Those with the love that commands compassion
obtain a nature of individual contemplation
and having attuned themselves previously to compassion,
they decrease disharmony and obtain purity.

The benefits of harmonious causes are twofold:

Through creating harmonious causes, you act only in this way;
your experience is free from disharmony and you obtain joy.

Through creating harmonious causes, you always generate meditations on the Four Immeasurables. As your experience is in harmony with the Immeasurables, it is never associated with harmful mind, harmful deeds, displeasure, attachment, or hatred.

The benefits of influence or dominance:

The dominant effect is that you are
born in a delightful, joyous, and harmonious land.
Where the people are ornamented by wealth and balance.

Due to love, you are born in a delightful land, due to compassion, you are happy, due to joy, the land is full of medicinal herbs and flowers and wealth of all good things, due to equanimity, you are born in a place where people are harmonious and never harmful.

The benefits of action. For beings:

Due to your actions,
the four increase and develop,
and the benefit of both self and other
is spontaneously fulfilled.

From meditating on the Four Immeasurables, through merit that increases, you achieve happiness and well-being.

Appendix

Notes

Now that I Come to Die

1 — This verse contains an allusion to the three Kayas: Dharmakaya (chos-sku), Sambhogakaya (longs-sku), and Nirmanakaya (sprul-sku). To paraphrase Dr. Guenther's original gloss on these terms: Being, which, as Dzogchen philosophers knew, is not an entity, is likened to the open sky and is experienced as intrinsic meaningfulness (chos-sku); this meaningfulness radiates like the sun, conveying something of this intrinsic meaningfulness experienced empathically (longs-sku). And just as the sun is the source of life for individual life forms, this charismatic activity gives meaning to each individual life form so that it is felt to have meaning (sprul-sku). For further philosophical implications of these terms, see *Kindly Bent to Ease Us*, Part 1, ch. 13.

2 — Kushinagara, also spelled Kushanagara and, in Pali, Kusinara, is the name of a city in ancient India. Nearby, the Buddha passed away.

3 — The term 'unique occasion and right juncture' is Dr. Guenther's translation of the Tibetan *'dal byor* (see *Kindly Bent to Ease Us*, Part 1, pp.6-7 and p. 254, note 13). In other translations this term is sometimes rendered as 'freedom and good fortune' (see, for example, Zhechen Gyaltsab, *Path of Heroes*, Part I, pp. 54 ff. Dharma Publishing 1995)

4 — The three trainings are: 1/ Self-discipline, without which nothing is possible; 2/ concentration, leading to the 'feeling' of wholeness as basis for a fresh vision of reality; and 3/ discriminative appreciation, which helps remove fictions about reality. They are linked to the division of the Canon into the 'Tripitaka', the 'three collections' or 'baskets' (see *Crystal Mirror* VI, pp. 50 ff., Dharma Publishing 1984).

5 — 'Limpid clearness and consummate perspicacity' is Dr. Guenther's translation for Bodhicitta (*byang-chub-sems*), usually translated 'enlightenment'. (See *Kindly Bent to Ease Us*, Part 1, pp. 123 ff. and p. 257, note 19.)

6 — 'Pristine cognition' is the translation of the Tibetan term *ye-shes* (see *Kindly Bent to Ease Us*, Part 1, p.257, note 18).

7 — Dr. Guenther's decision to capitalize the word 'Mind' attempts to indicate that we deal not with a 'thing' mind, but with the intrinsic cognitiveness of 'intelligence' of Being.

8 — 'Fields of merit, whether inferior, mediocre or superior' refers to the Shravakas, Pratyekabuddhas, and Bodhisattvas.

9 — The three sublime strata are Dharmakaya (chos-sku), Sambhogakaya (longs-sku), and Nirmanakaya (sprul-sku). (See above, note 1.) The twofold aim is the unity of the 'in-itself' and the 'for-others'.

10 – The thirty-seven facets of self-growth (or thirty-seven wings of enlightenment) are divided according to the Five Paths: The preparatory stage; the linking-up stage; the stage of seeing; the stage of cultivation; and the stage of no-more learning. (For a more detailed account see *Kindly Bent to Ease Us*, Part 1, pp 241 ff.)

11 – See note 10.

12 – 'The six kinds of beings' are gods, demi-gods, denizens of hell, hungry ghosts, human beings, and animals. (See *Kindly Bent to Ease Us*, Part 1, pp. 29 ff.)

13 – See note 1.

14 – One of the many names of Longchenpa.

The Four Immeasurably Great Catalysts of Being

15 – See above, note 5.

16 – As Dr. Guenther explains, 'emotions' are a malfunction of pristine cognitions, which alone presents the qualitatively authentic character of Being. Once the malfunctioning occurs, 'equality pristine cognition' shows up in inauthentic, fictitious being, as 'arrogance', which is

an ego-inflation, and the 'meaningfulness-continuum pristine cognition' as spiritual darkness. The catalyst for restoration of pristine cognition is 'equanimity'. Similarly, 'individualizing pristine cognition' turns up as a clinging to whatever has been selected, and this becomes a person's 'world'. Here 'compassion' is the catalyst. The 'mirror-like pristine cognition' takes on the character of 'aversion', which is to be broken down by 'love'; and the 'pristine cognition that things just are' appears as 'envy', the desire that things should have been otherwise, an emotion to be broken down by 'joyfulness'.

17 — The first stratum is chos-sku (Dharmakaya); the second is gzugs-kyi sku, which comprises both longs-sku (Sambhogakaya) and sprul-sku (Nirmanakaya).

18 — Obscuration by emotional vagaries and obscuration by notions about the knowable.

Longchenpa Sadhana

For centuries, the anniversary of the Parinirvana of the Great Omniscient One, Kunkhyen Longchenpa, was the occasion for extensive ceremonies at Nyingma monasteries in Tibet. In 1959, when the Chinese army took over the government of Tibet, religious observance was discouraged throughout the land, and this ceremony also was greatly restricted.

During the 1960s and 1970s, as Tibetan refugees worked to re-establish their culture in India and the Himalayan regions, ceremonies were gradually revitalized within the four major Buddhist schools. Inspired by the teachings of his guru, Jamyang Khyentse Chokyi Lodro, Tarthang Tulku sought to revitalize important ceremonies and revitalize traditional Buddhist holy places. His efforts led to the founding of the Monlam Chenmo, the annual World Peace Ceremony, first observed by tulkus, monks, lamas, and nuns of the Nyingma tradition at Bodh Gaya in 1989. This ceremony was followed by similar ceremonies observed by the Kagyu, Sakya, and Gelugpa traditions at Lumbini and Sarnath.

In 1995, Tarthang Tulku Rinpoche, building on the success of the Monlam Chenmo, sought to re-establish the traditional Longchenpa sadhana at Sarnath, site of the Buddha's first teaching and the founding of the Buddhist Sangha. Invoking the blessings of the enlightened lineage, this ceremony carries religious and symbolic significance for the continuation of the highest teachings of the Nyingma tradition.

Tarthang Tulku later shared his memories of the traditional ceremony as observed for centuries in Tibet:

"When I was a young man studying the Dharma in Tibet, I was fortunate enough to receive teachings from the famed Angyur Rinpoche. Each year when the time came for the Longchenpa sadhana, Angyur Rinpoche would celebrate it extensively in honor of his father, the great Adzom Drukpa. For three weeks all other activity ceased while three hundred lamas prepared for and participated in the ten-day ceremony.

"A famous aspect of these annual ceremonies was the torma, the ritual butter offerings prepared by the monks. The sadhana took place in February, at a time when it was bitterly cold. Even though the temperature at that time was invariably close to or below freezing, the torma, which were unusually large, gave off a special kind of nectar that was almost as thick as honey, Each year this nectar was collected and used for healing and other purposes. Many miracles were attributed to it.

"I myself witnessed this happening and tasted the nectar that gathered. Having received such an introduction, I have always considered the time of Longchenpa's Parinirvana deeply auspicious.

"In the 1960s, a few years after arriving in India, I resolved to honor this sacred time at Sarnath, and traveled there together with my Dharma brothers, Khenpo Thubten Mewa, Sangye Lama, Tsongdru, and the brother of my teacher Bodpa Tulku. We pitched a small tent there and practiced together for several days.

"The memory of this experience inspired me to reestablish the Longchenpa sadhana in 1995. Since the anniversary of Longchenpa's Parinirvana falls in late January to mid-February, shortly after the World Peace Ceremony, participants in the Monlam Chenmo traveled directly from Bodh Gaya to this ceremony in Sarnath.

"I feel it is a great blessing that the World Peace Ceremony and the Longchenpa sadhana can be held each year to strengthen the Sangha and to offer the world the benefits of the Sangha's prayers and devotion. It is doubly beneficial that these ceremonies can be offered at two of the four great holy places, Bodh Gaya, where the Buddha first manifested enlightenment in the world, and at Sarnath, where the enlightenment of the first disciples brought the Sangha into being, establishing the foundation for the Three Jewels of Buddha, Dharma, and Sangha to continue long in our world."

The 1995 ceremony, held from February 15-18, was attended by 1,492 tulkus, monks, lamas, and nuns. The central prayer recited at the ceremony was the Bla-ma'i sgrug-pa thig-le rGya-chen.

The Longchenpa Sadhana was held in Sarnath from 1995 through 2001, attended each year by 1,000 to 2,000 tulkus, monks, lamas, and nuns and a growing number of laypersons from eastern and western lands. However, in the year 2002, when an unusually large number of practitioners gathered in Bodh Gaya for the Kalacakra ceremony, the Longchenpa ceremony was held at the Mahabodhi Temple instead, for the benefit of those who might have difficulty traveling to Sarnath. Since 2002, the Longchenpa ceremony has been observed annually in Bodh Gaya.

An Invitation to Connect with the
Blessings of Longchenpa

The 14th annual Longchenpa Sadhana, to be held in Bodh Gaya, India in 2008, marks the 700th anniversary of Klongchen-pa's Parinirvana. Anyone wishing to make a special connection with the blessings of this great enlightened master is welcome to attend.

Tibetans traditionally make offerings for major ceremonies out of devotion to the Buddha, Dharma, and Sangha and their wish to promote peace and harmony. Support for ceremonies conducted in India by the Nyingma Sangha and participants from eastern and western countries alike invites blessings on self and others and is intrinsically meritorious.

Dharma Publishing International, through its program Adopt a Tibetan Book, encourages donors wishing to participate in this practice to contribute to the Longchenpa sadhana or the World Peace Ceremony. Funds are used for the printing of books and daily offerings to the monks and nuns. Contributions may be made directly to Adopt a Tibetan Book, which will take responsibility for their distribution according to the sponsor's wishes.

Adopt a Tibetan Book
35788 Hauser Bridge Road
Cazadero, CA 95421
707-847 3717
www.adoptabook.us

Bibliography

mDzod-bdun (The Seven Treasures)

Yid-bzhin rin-po-che'i mdzod

Man-ngag rin-po-che'i mdzod

Chos-dbyings rin-po-che'i mdzod

Grub-mtha' mdzod

Theg-mchog mdzod

Tshig-don mdzod

gNas-lugs mdzod

Mun-sel sKor-gsum

dPal-gsang-ba'i-snying-po-de-kho-na-nyid-nges-pa'i-rgyud-kyi-'grel-pa-phyogs-bcu'i-mun-pa-thams-cad-rnam-par-sel-ba

dPal-gsang-ba-snying-po'i-spyi-don-legs-par-bshad-pa'i-snang-bas-yid-kyi-mun-pa-thams-cad-sel-ba

dPal-gsang-ba-snying-po'i-rgyud-kyi-bsdus-pa'i-don-ma-rig-pa'i-mun-pa-thams-cad-sel-ba
rgyal-ba'i-dbang-po-kun-mkhyen-klong-chen-rab-'byams

sNying-thig Ya-bzhi

Bla-ma-yang-tig

Bi-ma- snying-thig

mKha'-'gro-yang-tig

mKha'- 'gro-snying-thig

Zab-mo-yang-tig

rDzogs-pa-chen-po Ngal-gso-skor-gsum

rDzogs-pa-chen-po-sems-nyid-ngal-gso

rDzogs-pa-chen-po-sems-nyid-ngal-gso'i-'grel-pa-shing-rta-chen-po

rDzogs-pa-chen-po-sems-nyid-ngal-gso'i-'grel-pa-shing-rta-chen-po'i-bsdus-don-gyi-gnas-rgya-cher-dbye-ba-padma-dkar-po'i-phreng-ba

rDzogs-pa-chen-po-sems-nyid-ngal-gso'i-gnas-gsum-dge-ba-gsum-gyi-don-khrid-byang-chub-lam-bzang

rDzogs-pa-chen-po-bsam-gtan-ngal-gso

rDzogs-pa-chen-po-bsam-gtan-ngal-gso'i-bsdus-don-pundarika'i-phreng-ba rDzogs-pa-chen-po-bsam-gtan-ngal-gso'i-'grel-pa-shing-rta-rnam-par-dag-pa

rDzogs-pa-chen-po-bsam-gtan-ngal-gso'i-don-khrid-snying-po-bcud-bsdus

rDzogs-pa-chen-po-sgyu-ma-ngal-gso

rDzogs-pa-chen-po-sgyu-ma-ngal-gso'i-bsdus-don-mandarava'i-phreng-ba

rDzogs-pa-chen-po-sgyu-ma-ngal-gso'i-'grel-pa-shing-rta-bzang-po

rDzogs-pa-chen-po-sgyu-ma-ngal-gso'i-don-khrid-yid-bzhin-nor-bu

Ngal-gso-skor-gsum-gyi-spyi-don-legs-bshad-rgya-mtsho rdzogs-pa-chen-po-ngal-gso-skor-gsum-gyi-dkar-chag-pad-ma-stong-ldan

RANG-GROL SKOR-GSUM

rDzogs-pa-chen-po-sems nyid rang grol

rDzogs-pa-chen-po-sems-nyid-rang-grol-gyi-lam-rim-snying-po'i-don-khrid

Sems-nyid-rang-grol-gyi-gsol-'debs

rDzogs-pa-chen-chos-nyid-rang-grol

rDzogs-pa-chen-po-chos-nyid-rang-grol-gyi-don-khrid-yid-bzhin-snying-po

rDzogs-pa-chen-po-mnyam-nyid-rang-grol

rDzogs-pa-chen-po-mnyam-nyid-rang-grol-gyi-don-khrid-rin-chen-snying-po-zhes-bya-ba-shin-tu-gsal-ba

BIOGRAPHIES

Longchenpa has been the subject of a great number of biographies by outstanding masters. Among them were Zhechen Rabjampa and Gyurme Kunzang Namgyel, who both prepared catalogs of Longchenpa's writings that contain many facts concerning Longchenpa's life. Mewa Khanchen's *Life Story of the Omniscient One* is also an important resource for the life story of this great master.

Biography of Longchenpa

Originally produced for distribution at the World Peace Ceremony, this beautiful volume includes the extensive eleven-chapter biography of Longchenpa composed in prose and verse by Lama Mipham's renowned disciple, Mewa Khanchen, together with a guide to the writings of Longchenpa written by the founder of Zhechen Monastery, the famed master Rabjam Gyurmey Kunzang Namgyel.

This text, in typeset Tibetan script, includes a full-color thanka of Longchenpa and ornamental art pages, bound in orange Lexotone and gold-stamped with the Wheel of the Dharma.

Printed on acid-free paper. 626 pages. $49

Acknowledgments

Translations of the three teachings in this collection have previously appeared in the following publications:

Now that I Come to Die — Longchenpa's parting injunctions, translated with commentary by Herbert V. Guenther, were first published in *Crystal Mirror* V (Berkeley: Dharma Publishing, 1977; second revised edition 1991 published as *Lineage of Diamond Light*). The positive sentiment of this injunction calls to mind a line by British poet Robert Browning, which is why the translator chose it as the title.

The Four Immeasurably Great Catalysts of Being was originally published as chapter seven of the first volume of the English translation of the Ngal-gso-skor-gsum ("Trilogy of Finding Comfort and Ease), published in three volumes as *Kindly Bent to Ease Us* (translation and commentary by Herbert V. Guenther, Dharma Publishing 1975-76).

Longchenpa's Verses and Commentary on the Four Immeasurably Great Catalysts of Being was originally published in *Gesar Magazine* 1992 (The translation has been adapted by the Yeshe De translation group from the Ngal-gso-skor-gsum and its auto-commentary.) The original translation. published as "Four Immeasurables, Verses and Commentary," was serialized as follows: Vols. 10(4):4–7; 11(2):7–12; (3):6–10; (4):6–10; 12(1):12–14; (2):19–22; (3):6–12.

Index

Abhidharma, 12
absence, 99, 110
absolute, 69
    sense, 95
acceptance, 47, 60
accumulations,
    two, 117
action, 11, 20, 23, 30, 58, 91, 118-120
    appropriate, 50, 51, 81
    charismatic, 42, 80, 125
    karmic, 55
    meritorious, 24
    shopa, 11
    three, 94
    virtuous, 104
Adibuddha, 11, 23
Adopt a Tibetan Book, 133
Adzom Drugpa, 20, 23, 130
affirmation, 47, 69,
affliction, 46, 53
age, 17, 21
    old, 75, 94, 103
agent 30, 67, 80
    four cardinals 69

agitated, 77
agitation 114
Ah, letter, 34
aim,
    twofold, 50, 126
alertness, 55
    circumspect, 55
alienate, 117
All-knowing, 17, 30, 33, 109
anger 92, 101
Angyur Rinpoche, 130
animal, 92, 127
antidote, 113-115
Anuyoga Tantra, 11, 19
apathy, 68
appearance, 25, 47, 57, 105
application, 112
appreciation, 50-51
    discriminative, 126
Arhat, 20
arrogance, 80, 127
aspect, 20, 27, 90, 114
    outer and inner, 82
    three, 54, 75, 81

aspiration, 53
Atisha, 16
Atiyoga, 11-16, 19, 21, 24, 29
atoms, 98
attachment 45, 49, 53, 71-73, 77, 78, 88-91, 93, 100, 113-114, 119
attainment, 22, 24-25, 100, 107
attitude, 71, 96
    observable mental, 70
audience
    nine different kinds, 11
Avalokiteshvara 20
aversion 53, 128
awakened,
    being 31, 95
    energy, 32
    state, 28
awareness, 51, 95
    discriminating, 46
    nature of human, 22
    pristine, 51

balance, 119
baskets,
    three, 126
behavior,
    calm, 56

Being, 41-46, 57, 60, 61, 67, 69, 74, 79-81, 87, 125-126, 127
    bitendential value of, 79
    openness of, 81
being, 9, 17, 20, 31, 33, 49, 51, 52, 55-56, 62, 72, 74, 75-76, 90-93, 96-99, 101-106, 110-111, 113, 120
    and non-being, 107
    awakened, 95
    fictitious, 39, 127
    human, 22, 24, 31, 34, 67, 92, 127
    inner, 45
    living, 42, 69, 74, 76, 82, 88, 97, 99
    merit of the, 101
    sentient, 71, 74, 90-93, 96-100, 102-105, 109-110, 117
    six kinds of, 52, 92-93, 127
    wholeness of, 33
benefit, 25, 42, 51, 59-62, 88-90, 95, 97, 100, 117, 119-120, 131-132
Bhutan, 18
bibliography, 134
biography, 137
birth, 16, 22, 73, 75, 77, 94-95, 103, 110

Bla-ma'i sgrug-pa thig-le rGya-chen, 132
blessings, 19, 31-33, 35, 130-133
bliss, 45, 47, 50-51, 53, 55, 59-61, 97
Bodh Gaya 14, 129, 131, 132
Bodhicitta, 126
Bodhisattva, 9-11, 15, 17, 20, 52, 126
Bodhisattvayana, 10
Bodpa Tulku, 131
body, 15, 23, 27, 34, 35, 44, 44, 77, 99, 101, 104, 112
Buddha, 10-12, 17, 32-34, 52, 56, 58, 97, 107-125, 129, 131-132
    future, 81
    qualities, 80
    sons, 82
    teachings, 9, 111
Buddhaguhya, 12
Buddhahood, 59, 79
Buddhism, 28, 41, 130
    Tibetan, 9, 22
byang-chub-sems, 126

calm, 70-74, 77, 91
    inner, 58
calmness, 70
caring, 52, 104,

catalyst, 128
    of being, 67, 89, 127
cause, 49, 69-70, 78, 81, 94, 113, 118-119
cause and effect, 12, 25, 29, 77, 94
ceremony, 16, 129-132
    world peace, 129-138
chakra, 34
change, 22, 48
Charya Tantra, 10
Chetsun Senge Wangchuk, 15
child, 17, 44, 52, 74, 97, 118
Chimpu, 15-19
Chogro Lui Gyeltsen, 13
chos-nyid, 95
chos-sku, 125, 126, 128
clinging, 47, 58, 68, 128
cognitiveness,
    intrinsic, 126
collection,
    three, 11, 126
comfort, 18, 82
commitment, 12, 58
compassion, 31-32, 42, 49, 52, 67-70, 74, 76-81, 87-88, 102-109, 113-116, 119, 128
    Lord of, 60
    non—referential, 76

complacency, 48
composure, 76
concentration, 50, 77, 102, 126
concepts, 26, 29-31
concern, 44, 55
condition, 11, 31, 113
    necessary, 81
conduct, 47, 56
confidence, 35
confusion, 31-32
conqueror, 118
consciousness, 12, 25, 92, 99, 115,
    human, 27-30
    pure, 98
contemplation, 17, 46-47, 58, 73, 87-92, 96, 102, 109-113, 119
contentment, 57-58
craving, 43, 58
cultivation, 46, 59, 73-78, 92-100, 104, 110, 127,
cupidity, 79

daka, 60
dakini, 17, 60
dal 'byor, 125
Dangma Lhungyi Gyeltsen, 15
darkness, 18, 45, 50, 80

    mental, 72
    spiritual, 128
death, 41, 58-59, 61, 75, 94, 103
dedication 54
deity, 17
    inner, 88
delight, 53, 55, 96-97, 100-101, 114, 119
deliverance, 50, 53, 57, 61, 70, 75, 81
    road to, 44, 69
delusion, 106
demi-gods, 127
denial, 47
denizens,
    of hell, 127
desire, 31, 51-52, 55, 68, 70, 72, 75, 91, 103, 128
    cause of, 118
despair, 114
devotion, 24, 35, 44, 53-54, 131-132
Dharma, 9-13, 17-18, 21, 111, 118, 130-132
    eyes, 24
    Publishing, 18, 125, 133
    wheel of, 10, 138
Dharmadatu, 25-28
Dharmakaya, 11-12, 19, 22, 24, 27, 30, 35, 37, 125-126, 128

Dharmapalas, 16-17
Dharmata, 95
direction, 70, 97
    ten, 74
disciple, 12, 19, 23-24, 58, 61, 131, 138
    twenty-five, 13, 15-16
discipline, 20
    natural 56
discrimination,
    appreciative, 81
disease of, 45
disinterest, 90
distractions, 59
division,
    subject-object, 47-49
Do Khyentse Yeshe Dorje, 20
doubt, 46
dream, 48, 57
Drime Odzer, 10
Dromtonpa, 16
drop, 15
duality, 47-48, 94-95
    non, 48
dying, 60
mDzod-bdun, 18
Dzogchen, 10-11, 14, 19, 23, 25, 29, 125

ease, 17-18, 32, 41, 82, 115, 125-127
effect,
    dominant, 79, 119
effort, 49, 51-52, 55, 59-61, 82, 129
ego,
    inflation, 127
elation, 70
elements, 31, 99
    six, 98-99
embodiment, 19, 27, 30, 32, 35, 72
    spontaneous, 80
emotionality, 45, 90, 91
emotion, 31, 45, 51, 55, 57, 72, 90-91, 127-128
emptiness, 47, 98, 107
empty, 99
enemy, 44, 51, 71, 88-89
energy, 22
    awakened, 32
enlightenment, 10-11, 21-22, 25, 31-33, 51, 97, 107, 117-118, 126, 131
    heart of, 110
    nature of the Buddha, 32
    path of, 286 33
    seed of, 118
    thirty-seven wings of, 127
envy, 77, 80, 128

equanimity, 53, 67-70, 73, 77-78, 80, 87-96, 113-116, 120, 128
equipoise, 105
essence, 30, 34-35, 42, 44, 99-100, 110
   immortality/giving, 59
   no abiding, 42
evenness, 53
Excellent Ones, 37
exertion, 44
existence, 25-27, 41, 61, 71, 73, 78, 110
   bodily, 44, 75
   or non existence, 28, 111
   substantial, 98
existent,
   non, 99, 111
expectations, 47, 51

facticity, 48, 80
faith, 54
false, 14, 100
father, 71, 88, 96, 102-103, 130
   Three Founding, 9-11
fearless, 59
   feeling, 31, 67, 97-99, 126
      holistic, 51
      four, 67-68
      neutral, 115

focus, 10, 23, 58, 88, 91-93
   objective, 98, 109-110, 114-115
   object of, 114
forces,
   growth/aiding, 67
form, 99, 109, 117
   is formless, 27-28
freedom, 70, 90, 93
freedom and good fortune, 125
friend, 43, 59, 71-75, 77, 88-92, 103, 113
   spiritual, 103
fruit, 95, 100
fruition, 47
frustration, 44, 49-50, 68, 70, 75
fundamental properties,
   four, 67

Garab Dorje, 11-12
Gelug, 22, 129
generosity, 55
God, 28, 31,
gods, 74, 78, 80, 96-97, 109, 117, 127
goodness, 49, 62, 78
grasping 27, 94-95, 106
Great Omniscient One, 129
guide, 44, 47, 138,

146   *Index*

guilt, 32
Guru, 44, 59, 129
    Maha, 34
growth, 67
    spiritual, 69
Gyelmo Yudra Nyingpo, 13
Gyud Bum,
    The Hundred Thousand
    Tantras, 11

happiness, 48-49, 58, 68-70, 74, 76, 78-79, 91, 96-97, 104, 109-110, 114, 118, 120
happy, 53, 56, 61, 72, 74, 76-79, 109, 112, 118-119
harm, 89, 118
harmonious, 119
hatred, 31, 44, 71-73, 79, 88-91, 100, 119
hearing, 100
heart, 15, 22, 32, 37, 54, 56, 59, 75, 104, 110
    chakra, 34
    nying', 15
    to heart, 24
    opening, 32
    enlightened, 37

helplessness, 68
holy places, 15, 129, 131
homage, 42
Hum, 34
human, 28, 30, 32, 97, 109, 117,
    awareness, 22
    condition, 31
    mind, 24
    potential, 32
humanity, 31
hunger, 31, 75
hungry ghosts, 127

I, 94-95
identity, 32, 48
idleness, 44
ignorance, 72, 90
illusion, 110-112, 114
immeasurable, 81-82, 101, 104
    four, 67, 69, 77, 87, 115-120, 127
    great properties, 82
immortality, 23, 59
    elixir of, 45
impermanence, 21, 42
India, 9, 11, 14, 20, 125, 129-133
indifferent, 89
indolence, 44

injunctions, 41
inquiry, 30
inspection, 54
    for, 52
instruction, 14, 45, 88
    Guru's, 59
intelligence, 126
intermediate,
    state, 57, 61
intimacy, 31

Jamyang Khyentse Chokyi Lodro, 20, 129
Jamyang Khyentse Wangpo, 20, 23
jealousy, 92, 110
    absence of, 110
Jigme Lingpa, 19
Jnanagarba, 87
Jnanasutra, 12
Jnenendra, 30
joy, 35, 53-61, 68, 77, 87-88, 101, 108-110, 112, 114-119
    essence of, 110
    object of, 110
    qualities of 112
    unobjectified, 114

joyfulness, 67-70, 76- 80, 128
    non-referential, 69

Kadampa, 16
    Deshek, 23
Kagyu, 129
Kaliyuga, 35
kalpa, 101
Kanjur, 10
karma, 12, 24, 25-27, 32, 61, 94
Katok,
    monastery, 23
Kawa Peltsek, 13
Kayas,
    three, 125
Khenpo Thubten Mewa, 131
Kindly Bent to Ease Us, 18, 32, 41, 125-127
kindness, 52, 71, 88, 103
klesha, 12, 25, 27
Klong-chen rab-'byams-pa, *see* Longchenpa, 41
knowable, 128
knowledge, 9, 15, 22, 30, 33-34
    field of vast, 16-17
    intellectual conceptual, 22
Kriya Tantra, 10

Kuntuzangpo, 20
Kushinagara, 42, 125

labeling, 46
language, 27-30
laziness, 44
learnedness, 45-46
lethargy, 117
Lhasa, 15
Lhasrung, 16
Lhatsun Namka Jigme, 19
liberation, 113
    path of, 45, 103
    seeds of, 118
life, 10, 16, 18, 21-24, 30-31, 42, 44, 53, 56-62, 78, 117-118, 125, 137
light, 59, 94
    pure, 34
lineage, 9, 14-16, 19-23, 25
    enlightened, 14, 20, 31, 130
    Longchenpa, 19
    of realization, 29
    transmission, 11, 13
    two streams, 13
logic, 18, 26-27
longs-sku, 125-126, 128
loneliness, 31, 67

Longchenpa, 10, 13-22, 24, 30-37, 41, 87, 127, 129-133, 137, 138
    Klong-chen rab-'byams-pa, 41
Kunkyen, 10, 17, 19-20, 129
Lopon Tensrung, 16
love, 31-32, 35, 44, 52, 67-70, 74, 77-80, 87-89, 95-104, 113-116, 119, 128
    non referential, 74
    superior, 97
Lumbini, 129

Madhyamika, 12
Mahapandita, 14
Mahasandhi, 11
Mahayoga, 11-12, 19
Maitreya, 18
malice, 71, 76, 88, 107
Manjushri, 9, 14-15, 34
Manjushrimitra, 12
Mantrayana, 9, 14, 20, 30
Marayas, 35
maturation, 78, 117-118
meaning, 15, 47, 59-60, 80, 125
    of life 59
    real, 42, 50, 56-59, 98

meaningfulness, 47, 54, 61, 80,
    continuum, 80, 128
    intrinsic 125
measure, 73, 92, 95, 110, 112
meditation, 15, 20, 24, 59, 61, 88-98, 100-120
merit, 54, 101, 117, 120
    fields of, 49, 126
Mewa Khanchen, 137-138
Milarepa, 20
mind, 12, 19, 22-23, 25-27, 29-35, 44, 47, 50-51, 54-58, 61, 69-74, 76-77, 82, 87-90, 92-93, 95, 100-102, 104, 107, 112, 114, 116, 126
    at rest, 51
    avaricious, 57
    caring and love, of, 104
    conceptual, 28
    control, 44
    conventional, samsaric frame of, 27
    darkness, of 50
    delusion of, 111-112
    dimensions, of 29
    disinterested, 90
    dynamic, 107-108
    equanimity, of, 89, 91
    functioning of the, 32
    guard the, 55
    harmful, 119
    history of, 28
    human, 24
    interpretations of, 29
    love, of, 101
    mastery of, 91
    mastery over, 90
    nine qualities of, 33
    no peace of, 75
    noble, 104
    ordinary, 26, 30, 33
    patterns of, 23
    samsaric, 30
    states of, 88
    tranquil, 103
Mind-as-Such, 73
Mipham, Lama, 138
mirage, 105, 106
mirror, 47, 79, 93-94, 128,
misery, 31, 48, 71-72
monastery, 15, 23
Monlam Chenmo, 129, 131
morality, 101
mother, 71, 74, 88, 96-97, 102-103
motivation, 99

Mount Kailash, 12
Mun-sel-skor-gsum, 18
Mune Tsenpo, 13
Muni, 100

Nagarjuna, 20
Nalanda, 9, 14
name, 99, 125
names and labels, 27
nature, 11, 20, 22, 32, 42, 61, 88, 93-95, 100, 105, 107, 119
Ngal-gso-skor-gsum, 18, 32
Nirmanakaya 125-128
Nirvana, 22, 25-26, 37, 62, 106-107
nobleness, 74
Nubchen Sangye Yeshe, 13
Nyak Jnanakumara, 13
Nyak-la Padma Dudul, 24
Nyang Ting nge dzin, 13
Nying-tig, 15, 20
    Khandro, 16
    Longchen, 19
    Vima, 15
Nyingma, 9-11, 17, 20, 22, 129-133

object, 47-48, 50, 93, 95, 98, 105, 110, 114, 119

of love, 68, 70, 96
obscurations, 82, 128
    two, 81
obstacle, 35
Oddiyana, 9, 14
Om, 34
openness, 74, 76, 81, 93
opportunity, 21, 56
ornaments, six, 37

Padma-las-'brel-rtsal, 61
Padmasambhava, Guru 9, 12-18
pain, 31, 90, 105, 117
pandita, 20, 22, 33
Pangen Sangye Gonpo, 13
parents, 52, 75, 113
Parinirvana, 21, 129, 131-132
participation, 67
passivity, 68, 114
path, 26, 32-33, 45, 50, 59, 80-81, 103-104, 107
    complete, 33
    five, 51, 127
    sacred, 107
    Sutra and Tantra, 82
    true, 103
Path of Heroes, 125

patience, 49
Patrul Rinpoche, 20
patterns, 23, 116
   human, 30
peace, 45, 75, 112, 133
   inner, 69, 82
   profound, 95
Pema Leytrel tsel, 16
Pema Sel, 13, 15-16
perception, 29, 99
perseverance, 53
   armor of, 52
perspective,
   relative, 26
perspicacity,
   limpid clearness and consummate, 45, 52-53, 55, 74, 76, 126
pleasantness, 74
pleasure, 76
positive,
   absolutely, 81
postulates,
   intellectual, 48
power,
   Buddha's, 56
   karmic, 21, 62

practice, 23-24, 26-27, 29, 33, 82, 87, 107, 115-116
   gompa, 11
prajna, 28
Prajnaparamita, 12, 17, 27, 89
Pratyekabuddha, 96, 104, 112, 126
Pratyekabuddhayana, 10
pray, 21, 34, 37, 62
prayer, 24, 37, 131-132
precious, 22
presence, 23, 34, 50, 57
   of ultimacy, 73
pride, 54
pristine cognition, 45, 79-80, 126-, 128
   equality, 80, 127
   individualizing, 80, 128
   meaningfulness-continuum, 80, 128
   mirror-like, 128
   knowing things to be, 80, 128
profound, 60, 73
   instruction in the, 45
properties,
   four immeasurably great, 77-82
propositions, 46, 73, 80

prosperity, 71, 78
sprul-sku, 125-126
psychology, 23, 33
purification, 100, 115
purity, 118-119
    primordial, 76
    state of, 117
pursuit,
    cause/dominated, 81
    goal/sustained, 81

qualities, 23, 33, 49, 52, 112, 116
    excellent, 43
    thirty-seven, 52
quintessence, 59-60

Rabjam Gyurmey Kunzang Namgyel, 138
rainbow body, 15, 23, 34
Rang-grol-skor-gsum, 18
real, 106, 110
reality, 25-30, 93, 111-112
    vision of, 126
realization, 19-20, 23, 25-29, 37, 41, 52, 78, 95, 100, 116
    Buddha's sacred, 33
    embodiment of, 30

highest, 23
realm, 21-22, 29, 47, 61, 97
    enlightened, 22-25
    formless, 28
    human, 11
    lower, 101-102
    of desire, 28, 117
    of form, 28
    three, 28
reason, 25-26
reference,
    objective, 69, 71, 74, 76-77
referential,
    non, 69
    objective, 76-77
    referential non, 70, 73-77
reflection, 93-95
refuge, 69, 81, 103
rejection, 47
rejoice, 54
renounce, 58
resentment, 44
result 14, 15, 73-78, 107, 112, 117-118
rhythm, 28

sadhana, 129-133
Sakya Pandita, 22

Sakya, 22, 129
Samantabhadra, 11
Sambhogakaya, 11, 125-128
sameness, 74, 89, 92, 95
samsara, 21, 25-26, 31-33, 37, 42, 44, 57, 75, 88, 90, 103, 107
    wheel of, 94
Samvrtti satya, 28
Samye, 15, 18
Samye-Pa, 18
Sangha, 130-133
Sangton Yeshe Lama, 13
Sangye Lama, 131
Saraswati, 17
Sarma, 17
Sarnath, 129-132
Sarvajñana, 34
self, 92-95, 98-100, 106, 112, 120
    nature, 94-95, 100
self-discipline, 49, 126
senses, 27-32
serenity, 67
seven treasures, 18
Shantarakshita, 9
shelteredness, 67
Sherab Dronma, 13
Shravaka, 96, 104, 112, 126

Shravakayana, 10
Shri Simha, 12
Shunyata, 25, 28, 30, 105
sickness, 75, 103
Siddhi, 35
sight, 100
six ornaments, *see* ornaments, six
skandhas, 93-94, 98, 106
solitary, 43
solitude, 58
Sonam Gyen, 16
sound, 28
space, ends of, 97-98
speech, 44, 55, 77, 101, 112
spirit, 21, 35, 62, 103
stability, 115-116
stage,
    link-up, 127
    of cultivation, 127
    of no-more learning, 127
    of seeing, 127
    preparatory, 127
steadfastness, 77, 116
steadiness, 118
strata,
    three founding, 82

    three sublime, 50, 52
    two, 54
    two founding, 81
stratum,
    of meaningfulness, 54
    of meaningful engagement, 79
    of meaning, 80
    founding, 80
    of the facticity of Being, 80
strength, 51
    inner 67
stupidity, 31
Subhuti, 89, 116
substance, 25, 28, 99
    or not substance, 28
success, 67
    spiritual, 52
suffering, 31, 52, 68, 72, 75, 77, 90, 102-105, 118
    freedom from, 70
    causes of, 90-91, 113
supplication, 51, 58, 61
Sutra, 17, 18, 22, 81
Sutrayana, 9, 14, 20, 30

Tanjur, 10

Tantra, 10, 17, 22, 30, 82
    hundred thousand, 11
    inner, 12-14, 15, 30
    inner and outer, 10-12
    Kunjed Gyalpo, 18
Tarthang Tulku, 35, 129-130
tattva, 88
teacher, 58, 80
teachings, 9-24, 30-33, 35, 111, 129-130
tendencies, 50, 91
    ingrained, 48
    latent, 72
Terdag Lingpa, 19
terton, 20
thatness, 88
thoughts, 27, 31,
    proper, 46
Three Jewels, 131
Tibet, 9, 11-18, 24, 129-130
tig, 15
time, 22, 59-60, 81, 88
    nature and dynamic of, 26
    past, present and future, 12
    three aspects of, 75, 81
    three, 94
trainings,
    three, 45, 126

Index   155

transcendence, 32, 112
transformation, 31, 35
transmission, 25, 29
transmutation, 25, 29
trilogy,
    of dispelling the darkness, 18
    of finding comfort and ease, 18
    of natural freedom, 18
Tripitaka, 126
Trisong Detsun, 9, 13-15
trust, 55-57
truth, 27-28, 31
    conventional, 33
    higher, 28
    of enlightenment, 21
    relative, 28
Tsongdru, 131
Tsongkhapa, 22
Turnings, Three, 10

ultimate, 93
    good, 117
uncertainty, 89
understanding, 24-26, 46-47, 73, 78
union, 34

unique occasion (and right juncture), 44, 125
unity, 37
    of Being and compassion, 76
    of love and Being, 74
universe, 31
unwholesomeness, 55-56
Uttaratantra, 18

Vairotsana, 12-14,
Vajra Guru, 34
Vajra Guru mantra, 34
Vajrasattva, 11
Vajrayana, 20
vehicles,
    nine, see yanas
Victorious One, 60
Vidyadharas, 20
view (tawa), 11
Vimalamitra, 12-19, 23, 34
vindictiveness, 76
violence, 72, 107,
    non, 108
virtue, 103-104
    non, 91
vision, 46
visualize, 34

wealth, 43, 47, 54-55, 57-60, 70, 75, 119
    inner, 77
welfare, 53, 69
    another's, 67-68
well-being, 67, 120
wholeness, 33, 41, 51, 126
wholesomeness, 51, 53, 55-56
wisdom, 27-31, 33, 117
wish, 97
Wish-Fulfilling Gem, 45, 51
world, 62
worldliness, 61
worldly,
    concerns, 44
wrongdoing, 58
Wu-t'ai-shan, Mount, 15, 23

Yanas, 12
    nine, 10-11
    three, 10
ye-she, 95, 126
Yeshe Nyingpo 87
Yeshe Tsogyal, 16
Yoga Tantra, 11

zhal-chems 41
Zhechen Gyaltsab, 125

Zhechen Monastery, 138
gzugs-kyi sku, 128